How to "Deal" Like a Millionaire

And Get Rich on Borrowed Money

HOW TO "DEAL" LIKE A MILLIONAIRE

$$$ $$$

AND GET RICH ON BORROWED MONEY

$ Charles L. Muse $

Parker Publishing Company
West Nyack, N.Y.

Library of Congress Cataloging in Publication Data

Muse, Charles L.
  How to deal like a millionaire, and get rich on
borrowed money.

  Includes index.
1. Business.   2. Credit.   3. Venture capital.
I. Title.
HF5386.M858   658.1'522   79-24394
ISBN 0-13-404657-9

Printed in the United States of America

DEDICATED TO MY WIFE, WANDA
AND MY SON, BUZ,
WHOSE ENTHUSIASM AS ENTREPRENEURS
PROMPTED THE WRITING OF THIS BOOK

WHAT THIS BOOK
WILL DO FOR YOU

This is your future — We are entering the greatest era of fast money-making opportunities ever known in the history of our free enterprise system. Within the next few years, thousands of entrepreneurs will become millionaires, and you could be one of them.

It isn't necessary for you to be a financial genius to "deal" like a millionaire. This book is the insider's guide to riches — It contains the formulas that have been followed by the new millionaires in our country today.

By following these simple stepping stones to riches, you will start making money a hundred times faster than if you tried every "pie in the sky" scheme, or "hit and miss" idea that comes along.

You are going to be surprised how easy it will be to handle large sums of money, once you begin to "deal" like a millionaire and get rich on borrowed money.

The first section shows you how to recognize profit in every deal you make — how to plan to be a millionaire with a foolproof system — how you can take an inventory of your own money making skills and abilities — how to put in black and white your money making goals — and the exact plans to follow to put you on the road to "dealing" like a millionaire.

Then, you get down to the "nitty gritty" business of making money using "O.P.M." (other people's money). The next four chapters detail methods with which you may borrow like a millionaire and get rich using little known secrets to obtain money from your banker. They show you how to take over going businesses with no cash out of pocket, and how to decide how much money you need, with your own tailored plan to repay.

Chapters 5 through 8 detail how millionaires raise money for their new money-making ideas, and how you can obtain free information on new "deals" before they reach the general public.

You quickly move into practical and proven steps to set up your own million dollar business — with tricks of the trade outlined for you.

You are then introduced to stories culled from confidential business loans that proved to be bonanzas for their borrowers. Pick out one and use it to skyrocket you to "dealing" like a millionaire.

The final chapters deal with items ranging from raising money from your own company stock sales to using little known secrets of lenders to sell a million dollars worth of real estate, even if you never owned a piece of property. From there, you will find ways to keep your money using legal tax avoidance and the new game of millionaires — tax havens — a perfect legal way to keep your money safe and paying double interest.

Throughout the book you will find foolproof systems for investing like a millionaire and not going broke while doing it. Everything you need to "deal" like a millionaire is put in a logical and practical order and, by adding your own ideas, you could make a fast fortune almost overnight.

I know that to "deal" like a millionaire means different things to different people, but I use the term in this book to mean building a fortune in the least amount of time, by using short cuts that have proven successful for those who have applied the principals of getting rich on borrowed money.

From the first to the last page I stress the positive note, which can move you *right now* to the big money and start you "dealing" like a millionaire.

It can happen to you.

With Best Wishes, Believe Me

Charles L. Muse

CONTENTS

11

How to "Deal" Like a Millionaire

And Get Rich on Borrowed Money

CHAPTER ONE

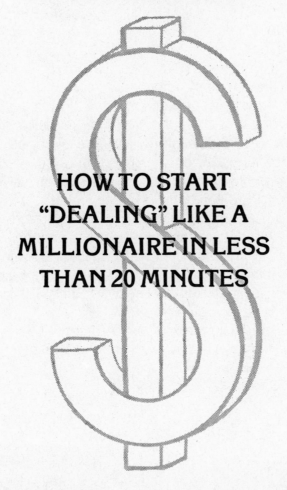

HOW TO START "DEALING" LIKE A MILLIONAIRE IN LESS THAN 20 MINUTES

Money-making is an art, and it can be learned just as easily as learning to drive a car or paint a picture. But, you must discover the basic techniques.

You could easily make a million dollars if you lived a thousand years, but the problem is that you only have approximately twenty or thirty years in which to make your fortune. To "deal" like a millionaire, you must take the short cuts to success.

It will take you less than 20 minutes to read this chapter, but during this brief period of time, I am going to tell you how you can start on the road to making more money than you ever dreamed possible — even without any money of your own.

There is only one person in ten who will put forth the effort to learn the principle of making money. The majority of mankind will lazily drift down the stream of time, barely making a living.

But, the well-defined steps for building a fortune, as outlined in this book, are not for the drifters. They are for *you*, the ambitious; for *you* who have the imagination and drive to take advantage of money making opportunities when they are presented to you. It is written for *you* who wish to "deal" like a millionaire and enjoy the thrill of making a profit using your own talent and ideas for making money.

Right here, let me remind you, that at some point while you are reading — it may be the first chapter or the last — you will suddenly grasp the "Millionaire's Secret" for making money.

It will almost jump from the pages. It will be so simple, you will wonder why you didn't discover it before!

$$ How Tony C. Used His Ambition Plus Borrowed Money to Get Million Dollar Results

Ambition plus borrowed money is the combination that puts you ahead. A man or woman with ambition can put an idea and an opportunity together, whereas others pass them by.

Tony C., of Tulsa, Oklahoma a projectionist for a local theatre, grasped at just such an opportunity. Tony was ambitious to "deal" like a millionaire.

One evening while working, he noticed that local merchants were running short spot commercials between feature movies. The idea flashed in his mind, "Why not advertise spot commercials on billboards at night with a movie projector? I can sell 60-second or five-minute spots of advertising, just as the local theatre boys are doing."

Tony owned a small pickup truck, but he needed money to buy a projector, which would cost in the neighborhood of $3,000. As I mentioned, he was ambitious, and he therefore set a goal.

His first stop was his bank. He obtained a loan to buy a special projector that he mounted on the back of his pickup truck, high enough to project an image across the street to the wall of a building.

Next, Tony printed up some cards showing his advertising rates per minute and began to contact local merchants. In one day, Tony had enough contracts for a week's showing.

He then found a prime location on a busy street. He approached the owner of the building and rented the wall space on which to project his ads. (He gave the store owner five minutes of free advertising on his own wall for the space.)

On the first night, when Tony began to flash ads on the side of the building in full color and full movie screen size, the street was filled with onlookers. His subscribers were delighted.

But thats not all — Tony's business has zoomed to three projection trucks, grossing over $1,000 each night.

Tony's *ambition*, along with his working partner "borrowed money," and our free enterprise system, has put him on the road to "dealing" like a millionaire.

There are lots of opportunities around, and you can find them. You probably have one in mind right now. They don't have to be unusual ideas like Tony's, but can be found in common business.

Here are a few of the most profitable small businesses in the world that you could start up with sound advice and borrowed money. I am going to show you how to obtain both from your banker without any money of your own, just your ambition.

Choose one for an example, and use it through-out the book to outline your fortune.

Tune-up shop	Secretarial service
Hamburger stand	Mail order business
Burglar alarm manufacturing	Pet cemetery
Flower vending	Car wash
Skateboard park	Hot dog stand
Plant shop	Pinball arcade
Liquor store	Mattress shop
Instant print shop	Health food store
Swap meet promoting	Pipe shop
Newsletter publishing	Coin-Op TV
Sculptures by computer	Homemade cake shop
Muffler shop	Bicycle shop
Popcorn vending	Mini warehouse
Sculptured candle making	Carpet cleaning service
Roller skating rink	Day care center
Pet shop	Donut shop
Paint & wallcovering store	Janitorial service
Tool & equipment rental service	Furniture rental store
Pet Hotel & grooming service	Soup kitchen
Import & export	Womens apparel shop
Auto parking service	Dry cleaning shop
Coffee shop	Self service gas station
Furniture store	Mobile restaurant
Employment agency	Salad bar restaurant
	Hobby shop
	Pizzeria

Every millionaire of today was filled with *ambition* when he started. The moment you lose your ambition, your progress in the money-making world ceases. Keep up the pace — the rewards are great.

Please remember, *ambition* cultivates chances. Here is a statement that will shock most people: *nearly every man is a gambler.* Yet, if you will stop and think, every move you make in a business deal is a gamble. You "bet" you will take in more money than you put out. The man with ambition to become rich is a gambler. The man who is content on a salary, and doesn't strive to increase his income is not a gambler.

Most men pride themselves on the ability to buy things cheaper, which means their incomes will go farther, never thinking that they could increase their earnings and buy the most expensive.

We know that any person in good health can earn a living, but the man who wishes to deal like a millionaire must work harder and be ready to grab every opportunity to make an honest profit.

For instance, Warren D. was a man who wanted more than just a living. He had a driving ambition to make a fortune before his 25th birthday. Warren was 18 years old when he first came into the bank to borrow $1,600 to buy an elaborate set of recording equipment.

A friend asked Warren to make a recording of his wedding and produce enough tapes for relatives of the bride. This was the birth of an idea that now grosses Warren over $100,000 per year.

Warren records speeches at Rotary Club luncheons, conventions, and all types of meetings where he can record lectures and sell cassette tapes.

Warren, at one seminar, sold 300 copies of the principal lecture, at $10 per copy. Not bad for an 18 year old entrepreneur.

He now has conventions that hire him to record every meeting, with a guarantee to purchase a certain number of cassettes.

Remember that you must get permission to record any conference or convention, but that usually isn't too difficult.

Don't overlook the fact that your Chamber of Commerce can give you dates of coming events.

All you need is a quality recorder, a cassette duplicator, and blank cassettes, and you are in business. And, as we mentioned, you need no cash out of pocket. See your banker and borrow other people's money.

Then follow your ambition to a lifetime fortune.

$$ How Ralph and Nancy K. Made Borrowed Money Work for Them

Right here, let me say people's attitudes towards borrowing money has changed since the days of the '30's and early '40's. We are a nation filled with borrowers.

Everyone from corporate presidents to the next door neighbor who borrows money to send his children to college. We have adopted the words of Artemas Ward, "Let us all be happy and live within our means, even if we have to borrow the money to do it."

We could add a phrase, "If we desire to deal like a millionaire, borrowed money is our only avenue to wealth."

There are sensible reasons for borrowing money. First, inflation reduces your dollar's purchasing power each year. So, when you repay a loan, you are using dollars that are worth less than those you borrowed. Second, you have a friend, "Uncle Sam," who pays a portion of the interest, because interest on borrowed money is tax deductable. If you are in the 50% tax bracket, the government picks up half the interest charge. If your bank charges you 10% interest, you are really paying only 5% out of your own wallet.

You may be shy about borrowing all you can on a new car or a house, but you can't argue with figures. For example, Ralph and Nancy K. recently moved to Oklahoma City from Davenport, Iowa. They had sold their home and had a nice sum of $40,000 in cash from the sale of their home in Davenport.

They found a beautiful ranch type home with a price tag of $75,000. When it came to closing the loan, Ralph wanted to put down half their money, $20,000, and make a large monthly payment. Nancy reasoned that they had $40,000 from the sale of their previous home, so why not put it all down to make the house payment lower.

It didn't take Nancy long to change her mind when she saw the figures. With Ralph's plan, they would have almost $4,000 in interest the first year that was tax deductible. With Nancy's plan, they had less than $1,500.

In other words, by just a few dollars more on a monthly payment, they could realize the larger interest which is tax deductible. In fact, it is the same as if Uncle Sam made two house payments each year for this couple. And, in addition, Ralph and Nancy were able to put the $20,000 they still have into a trust fund for their children's education.

In Chapter 2 I will show you how to use your banker to borrow money. It pays to borrow money. (I have one bank customer, a single girl, Donna F., who borrows $2,000 a year and never uses the money. She puts the money in a savings account and makes a payment each month. True, she loses a little interest each year, but she is building a bank rating to use as a credit reference for a large loan at another bank. Also, she has developed a forced savings plan.)

As I mentioned, it pays to borrow money if you use the funds to pyramid your own fortune. Borrowed money is the least expensive item you can use on your road to "dealing" like a millionaire.

$$ How Bill M. Used the Power of Borrowed Money to Take in $3,600 per Month

How does this work? Let's see how Bill M. used the power of borrowed money.

Bill was a postal employee who was very conservative. He wasn't a promoter, but he could see a dollar a long way off.

One evening, Bill came to my office to borrow $400 and requested a note payable in 90 days. The loan was granted.

Knowing Bill's conservative background, I couldn't understand why he wanted only 90 days to repay his loan. I was even more surprised, when 60 days later he walked into my office and paid his note in full, with ten dollar bills. He also had over $2,000 in cash that he deposited in a savings account.

The next day, Bill came to my office and again requested another $400 for 90 days, saying he had learned how to make a fortune with other people's money (borrowed money). How did Bill pick up $2,000 in 60 days with an investment of only $400?

It was simple: Bill had become a mail order buff. He had found an "Electric Mosquito Repeller." It is a small gadget that fits into your pocket or purse and has a miniature horn that produces a hum that puts mosquitoes on the run.

Bill had found a company that would sell him the units for $2.00. He was running space advertising in hunting and fishing magazines and was selling them by the hundreds.

Bill never, at any time, used any of his own money. He would take the $400 he borrowed and buy "mosquito repellers," and was selling them for $12 each — a gross profit of ten bucks apiece.

Every big fortune today was started with an idea and borrowed money. In Bill's case, this amount was peanuts compared to other entrepreneurs who have borrowed millions.

The principal, however, is the same — borrowed money is your working partner, and the only wage he demands is the interest you must pay.

On your way to "dealing" like a millionaire, it doesn't matter where you start, but when.

Now is the time to set a goal that works. Start thinking about the big money. The secret is to set a goal, then start to make it happen.

$$ How Ralph C. Set His $175,000 a Year Money-Making Goal That Works

Ralph C. was 28 years old with a desire to be rich. He had worked in a cleaning shop for four years, and had saved less than $1,000. His future seemed bleak. One evening he began to map out a way to own his own shop. It will please you to know that he now owns six shops that gross over $175,000 a year.

While searching my files for success stories to share with you, I asked Ralph if he would tell us how he set his goals. It is simple. You must make plans to become rich, and here is his formula:

If someone called you from Kansas City and said you had just inherited a gold mine, what would you do? First, you would begin to figure out how to get there. You would find out where Kansas City was located. Second, you would need to know just where you are. When you determined this, you would find the quickest route to your goal, Kansas City. You begin to make plans for the trip.

You must do the same thing on your road to riches. *You must make plans!*

You plan your life to reach your goal (wealth) as fast as possible. For example: Referring to our il-

lustration, let us say you live in California. Would
you go through Nevada, Utah and Colorado to Kansas
City to claim your fortune, or would you go through
Arizona, New Mexico, Texas and Oklahoma? You
would take the shortest route. *Plan the same way to
riches.* If Kansas City was your goal, think of each
state as a sub-goal you must reach on the way to your
main goal.

Think of your business in the same way. If owning a chain of stores is your goal, you must first own
one store. Improve it, take the profits and open the
second store. Take the profits from both the first and
second store and open a third store, and so on. This
is the formula that Ralph C. used to gross $175,000
in his own business.

Now, how did Ralph open his first store with less
than a thousand dollars? Our working partner, "Borrowed money" came to his rescue.

Before Ralph left his job at the cleaning store he
approached his banker and obtained a $4,000 loan
with the equity in his home as collateral. Ralph knew
that with a down payment on cleaning equipment,
a supply company would make arrangements for the
balance to be financed at their own commercial bank.

Now, with his $1,000 he leased a building, bought
office supplies, and within 30 days was in business
for himself.

Here is where Ralph put his formula to work:

He took the profits from his store and used the
$4,000 he had in his equipment to borrow another
$4,000. Using the same principle, his second store
was opened.

The last time I talked to Ralph, he was planning
to open his seventh store, just by repeating the
process. Ralph was dealing like a millionaire, and will
soon be one, simply using borrowed money.

You can do the same. All you need is a goal to
put you on the track to the big money.

LITTLE-KNOWN SECRETS —
HOW TO SET YOUR GOAL TO
MAKE YOUR FIRST MILLION

To deal like a millionaire and make a million, you must set down our goals in writing. Take a sheet of paper and write down your goal. Then write down the sub-goals you must travel through to reach your final goal. This will take time and thought, but I would imagine you have already begun to formulate plans in your mind. This is good.

To have a map to riches, you must write it down on paper.

1. List the type of business you would like to own.
2. List the kind of social life you want.
3. List the type of home you desire.
4. List the make of car you want to drive.
5. List everything you will have when you reach your goal.

I always keep a list of my goals on a nightstand near my bed. I read them before I go to bed, and again when I awaken. It keeps my mind on the road I must travel to reach my goal.

Now that you have written down your goals, you must take a look at where you are. You must know this before you can begin to travel on the road to your goal.

Write down exactly where you are: How much money do I have?; Where am I socially?; What kind of house I live in; What clothes do I wear; What type of work do I do? You must be honest with yourself for most of us have the tendency to overinflate our present circumstances.

After you have done this, you can compare your goals with your present station in life and see how

far you must travel to reach your goals. Now, you are
ready to write down your intermediate goals. These
are the goals you must reach first on your way to obtain your main goal.

Write down what you must change first. List the
things you must do to reach your first intermediate
goal. Then list what you must do from that goal to the
next one. What do you need to know? Where can you
get the information? *Write it down.* When you have it
all down on paper, you have a *complete road map to
riches, your goal.*

While writing all this down, your mind has begun to work overtime for you to make all these things
come to pass. Strange as it may seem, various things
start happening to aid you to riches once you have
written it down, and have honestly committed yourself to your goal.

At this point, we should set a speed limit or time
on how fast we wish to travel to our goal. Don't worry
about all things at once. Men on the way to wealth
know they must pace themselves. Take one sub-goal
at a time. You are going to be amazed at how fast you
begin to succeed and accumulate money. This is a
thrill you will never tire of.

I would like for you to know in advance that
when you start dealing like a millionaire, your life
style will change.

If your spare time is spent watching TV, or you
enjoy old cronies at the corner bar, you will find that
this doesn't satisfy you any longer. You will begin to
seek out the best restaurants, the best motels when
traveling, and your friends will be the ones who are
successful in their own fields.

When making big money, take time out to enjoy
your money. Instead of one vacation, take two or
three. My wife and I always do.

Sure, you may miss a few good deals, but you are

in a position to enjoy the freedom that comes with *making big money* — *fast*.

To deal like a millionaire, this is the best time in American history to make a start. Now is the time to start your trip on the road to riches.

EIGHT SECRET RULES MILLIONAIRES USE THAT GUARANTEE YOUR SUCCESS

You won't believe this, but surveys show that only 10% of the population really desires to be rich. The other 90% would rather watch TV or sleep. They have all kinds of excuses for their lack of ambition to make money. They fail to listen to those who have become rich. For instance:

J. Paul Getty's rules for riches are so simple that it is easy to understand them. I would like to acquaint you with them.

Mr. Getty was considered the world's richest man, so his words should have a ring of truth. When you read these rules to wealth, you may find them so simple that you tend to put them aside. *Don't make this mistake.*

These are the real "nitty-gritty" rules for getting rich. Don't push them aside; put them to work for you. We suggest you write them on 3 x 5 index cards and place them on your mirror where you can read them every morning before you set out for the day to make your fortune in this land where millionaires are made every day.

Remember, there is no easy road to riches, but with rules to guide you and a *desire to get rich,* your chances are greatly increased.

> *Rule #1.   To acquire wealth doday, you must be in your own business.*

Rule #2.   You must have a working knowledge
of the business when you start it and
increase your knowledge of it as you
go along.

Rule #3.   You must save money in your personal
life and in your venture as well.

Rule #4.   You must take risks both with your
own money and with borrowed money.

Rule #5.   You must not only learn to live with
tension, but seek it out.

Rule #6.   Build wealth as a by-product of your
business success. If wealth is your
only object in business, you will probably fail.

Rule #7.   Patience — This is the greatest business asset of all.

Rule #8.   Diversify at the top.

Mr. Getty was a billionaire. Do his rules sound
too simple? Let's examine each one.

First: Own your business. You might think an
executive, working for someone else and making a
$30,000 annual income is much better off than you
would be running your own business. Stop and think.
The executive would be hard pressed to double his
income in a lifetime. Taxes would eat up most of it.

You, as a small businessman, can expand your
business and income to unlimited opportunities. The
businessman, also, has many tax advantages.

To be frank about it, the guy with the ham-
burger stand has a greater long-range opportunity for
wealth than a man working on a fixed salary for someone else.

Second: Knowledge is self-explanatory. You
must know what you are doing. You must keep up
with the mass of new information that affects your
business.

Third: The ability to save money is tied to personal discipline. Do you have the willpower to deny pleasures in order to save money for future expansion of your business?

Fourth: Taking risks is essential in all business. The ability to stake your life savings or the future of your entire business on borrowed money is going to be needed time and time again. *Believe me,* as a banker, I have seen many men become wealthy using borrowed money wisely. Remember, all risks must be backed by good judgment and without any reservations.

Fifth: Seek out tension. This is the real secret to great and wealthy men. They love the game: they like the excitement of business. Money is just a way to keep score of their losses and gains. You must have this same attitude. The game filled with challenge and tension must be what you want.

Sixth: Wealth is a by-product. If you win, the money is always there — *it never fails.*

Seventh: Patience. This means you must wait for the right opportunity to make your move. Let your business grow naturally. Don't press your luck.

Eighth: Now, you are wealthy. Take your money and move into bigger and better games. You can decide just how wealthy you want to be.

These are a billionaire's rules for getting rich. Don't forget the old saying, *"To get rich, do as the rich do."*

HOW YOU, THE MAN — NOT THE PLAN — WILL MAKE YOUR FIRST MILLION

"It's important to have a plan, but there is no "master plan" that will make money for you without your own ambition and drive. When someone approaches you with a money-making opportunity, don't make your judgment on the basis of the plan, but on the man himself.

Any man who has a well-defined goal, keeps his eyes focused on the prize, pushes through all obstacles in his path, and uses all his creative energy in moving toward his goal, is well on the road to becoming wealthy.

We have seen men make money where it was belived impossible. For instance: James D. moved to a small town in upstate New York, to open a small cafe. He approached the president of the Chamber of Commerce in an effort to find a suitable location. The president informed him that the small town was overcrowded with restaurants, many of them were barely meeting expenses, and it would be impossible for the town to support another restaurant.

Yet, James D. opened his restaurant, and it was an instant success. I understand that he later bought out two of his competitors.

If it was just "the plan" that was making the money, all we would have to do would be to buy a set of plans and follow instructions to become rich.

The great world of money making is filled with failures as the result of copying plans.

When a business or investment deal is presented to you, do not invest your money because of the plan — but invest because you are the man.

THE SECRET WORD OF MILLIONAIRES THAT CAN MAKE YOU A FORTUNE

Profit is the secret word. Operate your money-making opportunity, whatever it may be, to take your profits quickly. This is the key that will open doors and lead you to a quick fortune.

Too many men get so involved in operating a business that they miss the chance to take their profits at the right moment. Profit-minded people keep their eyes open. They think before acting, then act.

I grew up on a farm, and when I was still a boy, my Dad taught me a valuable lesson about profit. Suppose, he told me, I bought a cow at a cattle auction for $200. And, while I was loading her into my pickup truck, a neighbor offered me $250 for that cow. Should I turn him down and hold onto that cow to try to get a still higher price later? If I did, my Dad told me, I'd be making a mistake. I should take the money quick and let the man have the cow.

Take your profit as soon as you can! Don't ever hold what you have for some possible "killing" later on. You may never get a second chance for profit.

In any business deal, pick up any small profits that come your way when they come. Small profits soon add up to big earnings. If you hold out, waiting for that "big deal", you may wait forever. This is a hard lesson for some entrepreneurs to learn. Life is too short and the future is too unpredictable for you to wait for tomorrow's profit. Don't miss any opportunity to make a profit right now! As soon as you learn this technique of money making, you're on the road to "dealing" like a millionaire.

HOW TO SIZE UP "THINGS" LIKE A MILLIONAIRE TO MAKE BIG MONEY FAST

Recently, at a board of directors meeting, we asked Gerald R. what contributed most to his money-making success. I was surprised at his answer, but later when I had time to reflect, I could see the wisdom and how it had helped him accumulate a fortune in real estate.

His answer was simple: *size up the situation* — I believe this is one necessary step on your climb to riches you overlook.

You must set aside some time each day to size

up things. Set aside at least one hour a day to devote
to looking over the day's happenings, and think about
your money-making plans for the next day.

Remember the old saying, "Birds of a feather
flock together," is only partly true. There are some
birds who live in flocks, but not the strong eagle. He
soars far above the crowd.

What about man? The same is true. We find some
men who live with the crowd, but not those who desire to deal like millionaires. They are the active men.
They are the leaders.

Bert Fields, a hardware store owner, made
friends easily, and his customers trusted and re-
spected him. Bert knew that men who like crowds
too much fill their time at crowded bars or country
clubs. They are never happy if left alone with only
their thoughts for company.

Bert, armed with this knowledge, associated
only with his family and a few close friends who could
help advance his business interests. And, above all,
he has learned to size up a situation. In fact, Bert has
a sign he hangs on his office door for one hour each
day, which reads: GONE THINKING. All his telephone calls are held up and he receives no visitors.

Bert told me one day at lunch, that during his
"Gone Thinking" hour, the idea came to him to buy
out his competitor. That very day he walked down the
block and made an offer to the competitor. And, to
Bert's surprise, the owner accepted. The terms of
the sale were drawn up the next day and Bert was on
the track to becoming a chain store operator.

As I mentioned, the man who desires to be a
millionaire spends his time sizing things up. He lis-
tens to those who have made their fortune. He reads
and studies, just as you are doing now. He has a
burning desire to know how to make more money and
will not let the crowd sidetrack him from his goal.

There is one thing missing in our capitalistic

society — there isn't a school or college that teaches a person the fundamental basics on "how to get rich."

But, the man who wishes to deal like a millionaire and get rich on borrowed money must learn that experience is the great teacher — Not just our own, but the money-making experience of others as well.

If there is a wealthy man in your community, size him up. Talk to him. One thing you will learn is that he has set aside some time to be alone; to reflect; to solve his own problems; to make plans on how to handle the money-making deals for the next day.

Right now, take out time to size up what you have just read, then set aside 20 minutes each day to be alone, to size up your deals just like a millionaire.

At the end of each day, you will be enthusiastic about your newly found way to think like a millionaire.

CHAPTER TWO

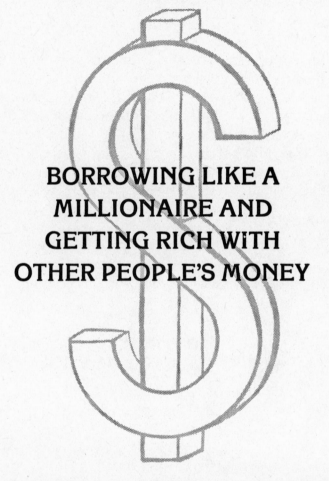

BORROWING LIKE A MILLIONAIRE AND GETTING RICH WITH OTHER PEOPLE'S MONEY

The inside secret of millionaires is simple enough — *why work for money when you can make "borrowed money" work for you!!!*

To start dealing like a millionaire you need a few dollars to start with. You may save out of your paycheck or draw funds from your business, but the fastest way is to use other people's money. Your own banker will tell you that you need to borrow money to make money and the smart thing is to start right now. He knows it is wise to borrow money for a home, **a** new car or major appliances, because they are likely to increase in value, while you have the use of them.

For example: Housing costs have increased at an annual rate of 10% or more, while mortgage rates have ranged from 8% and upward. You make money by borrowing rather than waiting until you have saved up to make the purchase.

It also makes good sense to borrow money to take advantage of large discounts on major appliances or furniture if you need them.

You should borrow money if the expenditure will help save or earn you money in the future. Suppose you live in a cold climate and you borrow money to winterize your home to save fuel or you go to a technical school to improve your skill in your own trade that will increase your income.

The thing to remember is that it takes money to make money, and you must learn to borrow just like a millionaire.

HOW YOU CAN "DARE" TO BORROW LIKE A MILLIONAIRE

When you approach your lender, keep in mind that you have a great idea for making money, and if you receive the money, assure your lender you will put forth hard work, will be honest and not disappoint those who have put trust in you and your money-making proposition. Let your lender know you are going to make money for him, also.

There is one point that is overlooked by hundreds of men who have set sail to "Deal" like a millionaire — they never borrow all the money they need. They ask for too little. *Always borrow all you can.* Borrow more than you think you will need. Even if you don't use it, you can always pay it back to the lender at a later date.

Keep in mind there are many expenses, even with

the best of planning, that will come up when you least expect them. For instance:

1. *Extra space in the yellow pages*
2. *Additional freight charges on shipped merchandise*
3. *The part-time employee when business booms*
4. *Attorney fees for forming a corporation*
5. *State and city license fees*
6. *Deposits on utilities*
7. *Janitorial supplies*
8. *Bookkeeping forms*
9. *Extra file cabinets*
10. *Even a coffee pot — coffee breaks are here to stay*

These are just a few. Other expenses will appear when you least expect them.

Make it a practice to borrow more than you need and you will be ready to meet, head on, any hidden expenses. But, many an entrepreneur has a horror of borrowed money. He wants to be safe. He does everything on a cash basis. He sails out on the ocean of business and finance in a small junket he calls "cash on hand" and never gets very far from the shoreline. In fact, he stays so close, that soon his dream boat hits a rock and sinks to the bottom, and that is the end of his business or money-making idea.

When you gain experience, you learn that all the rocks and reefs are near the shore, and that it is much safer far out in deeper water. If you can't sleep at night worrying over a debt, you should never try to deal like a millionaire. Find yourself a good, safe job — you may retire with a pension, but you will never have enjoyed the sport of being an entrepreneur.

As a banker, I must tell you this. If you want to

play your cards close to your vest and avoid all risk, you can never be a millionaire — unless you inherit it. Then, you may be able to keep it, but you will never make much money on your own.

The art of dealing like a millionaire has its risks. I can't point out all of them to you, and I don't know anyone who can. However, as a banker, I can give you a few valuable pointers in the art of taking calculated risks.

Here is a valuable tip I give all new loan customers who apply for money to invest in a risk venture. I explain that the difference between an entrepreneur and a gambler is intelligent risk. A gambler bets on a hunch or a friendly tip. The entrepreneur bets also, but he will weigh the facts at hand, judge his return against odds, then decide if he wants to risk his money. The successful entrepreneur puts his money up only when the *odds are in his favor.*

One of the biggest mistakes we can make is to spread our money too thin. I have seen people in such a hurry to get rich (they overlooked patience), that they have nickel and dime investments scattered around. They have stocks, coins, stamps and various and sundry investments. This is like sitting in six different kinds of games, not knowing the rules of any. They are just hoping to win. Blind hope doesn't make millionaires. If it did, the world would be full of them.

Please remember this — Nothing is more rewarding and profitable than an investment or business risk taken wisely.

Once you have made up your mind you can handle other people's money (borrowed money), then you should never hesitate to borrow all you can.

I know one man, Gerald C., in Dallas, Texas, who has a full time employee, a former bank examiner, whose duty is to contact banks and set up credit lines for his company. Ask any rich man in your city.

He will tell you he owes most of his success to borrowed money that was put to good use.

Recently, on a plane to Salt Lake City, the man next to me began to tell me about his tire recapping business. He was proud that he had built his business to an annual net income of $21,000.

This was done by saving a certain amount each year until he could *pay cash* for new tire vulcanizer equipment. Here is the kicker — this man had spent 10 years building his business to a $21,000 net income. If he had gone to his bank and borrowed $25,000, purchased new equipment and made annual payments on a loan, he could have built his business in half the time.

He had spent the prime of his life doing what he might have done in 5 years. We all overlook the time element.

There is nothing as cheap as borrowed money at bank rates. It is money and the man that makes the profit in every business or investment.

Money puts the profit-making factor in a venture. The man puts in the brains. If you are the man with the brains and imagination, the next thing you should do is get the money.

But that is not all. Try to borrow from a bank. If your business hits a rough streak, your banker will be easier to get along with than friends or relatives you could have borrowed from. No bank wants to lose a good borrowing customer. You are making money for them.

One little tip. A banker is trained to lend money. Also, he knows when to refuse a loan. If this happens, examine your business venture and find out why you were refused — It could save you thousands of dollars.

As I mentioned, if you can handle other people's money wisely, it is better to borrow like a millionaire and get rich with other people's money.

BORROW TO MAKE A PROFIT
— NOT INFLATE EGO

In my years in the banking and lending industry, we have seen many a man plunge his business into bankruptcy because he couldn't tell the difference in borrowing money to make a profit from borrowing money to inflate his ego.

Making a profit means you must expand your business when needed, while ego trips mean buying unnecessary things that don't add to the value of your business, but only show off.

If a farmer finds he is losing $10,000 a year for lack of a new tractor, he should go to his bank and borrow enough money to purchase the much-needed tractor.

If a clothier finds he could sell more men's suits if he had a larger inventory, then he should borrow to increase his supply.

But that is not all. A profitable business must grow to make large sums of money. But, that doesn't mean we should go overboard buying useless things just because our ego requires it. For example: You may need a set of drapes for the show window, but that doesn't mean they have to have gold threads.

Money should never be borrowed unless it can pay its cost (interest), plus a profit for you.

Recently my bank loaned a man money to open a meat market. Several days later, the butcher and I went to lunch together in the new luxury automobile he had purchased with money he had borrowed from a friend. He wanted advice on his new business. I wanted to tell him to sell his new auto and buy an extra meat counter to increase his sales.

I have also called on customers who lived in fine homes and even hired a gardener. But their business didn't have proper equipment and was on the brink of bankruptcy. If they had been good businessmen, they would have sold the fine house and fired the gardener, moved into a back room of the business building, and would have put the money back into the business to increase the assets. Then, they would visit their banker to borrow all they could and put their business on a profitable basis.

Believe me, as a banker, I have seen many men try to be lavish at the expense of their business ventures. It never works. Soon there is a "FOR SALE" or a "FORECLOSURE" sign hanging on the front door.

Not many people today would do as Hazel B. did. She slept in the back of her restaurant until it was a success. Nor Ray W., of Los Angeles, who lived in the rear of his shoe store until it was making a profit. Incidentally, he now owns 22 locations in the nation, and travels between each city in his own private airplane.

Make it a cardinal rule. Never take any money out of your business if it will be missed.

But that is not all. Don't get the idea that a new building or a larger building will increase business. I have two friends who would give anything to be back in their old locations.

There are times when the move can be justified, but if it is to satisfy your ego, or show off to friends or relatives, it will be a disaster.

Borrow to make a profit — *never* — *never* — to satisfy your ego.

HOW TO USE YOUR BANKER IN THE MONEY-MAKING JUNGLE

In the world of dealing like a millionaire, there are no cut and dried trails to follow. If there were, everyone would be a millionaire. The majority of people are lost in the jungle of money-making. However, there are a few men who understand the forest and will warn you of the dangers and sharp turns. The most knowledgeable is your *banker.*

Many a man has lost his way when he didn't heed the advice of his banker and listened to would-be friends.

The world is full of promoters waiting to transfer money from your pocket to theirs. These would-be friends and guides will tell you anything you want to know. But remember this — as soon as you open your wallet, hundreds will offer to help you to the end of the rainbow and offer to split the pot of gold. Really, it is like the blind leading the blind.

Some of the strangest things in the opportunity-seeking world: you will find a broke man who offers to make you rich; a sick man to make you well; a man in rags to show you how to be one of the ten best dressed men in America.

Take my word as a banker, very few people give a service or advice free. If it costs you nothing, that is about what it's worth. And, if he charges you a fee to show you how to get rich, don't you think he should act on his own advice?

Also remember — when he starts charging a fee, he becomes a broker and he has a motto; "Collect the fee in advance and let the customer take the risk."

I am not saying that all brokers are heartless, but I have never known one who would stay awake at night worrying about the losses of a customer.

A broker cannot guide you, because he collects a commission whether you win or lose. But there is a man whom you can rely on for sound financial advice — your banker.

Your banker is a protector of your money. He spends his lifetime studying national trends, as well as the economy of the local community. He knows when new businesses are coming to town, which stores are doing well, and the ones that are barely breaking even.

And, in addition to that, your banker can help you when you are in trouble financially. The good part is that he is paid a salary, not a commission, for his services.

From experience, I know that many customers of a bank never seek the advice of their banker until they are facing a loss or their business is in financial trouble.

Your banker has no reason to give you bad advice. If you seek advice from your banker, you will get information that can be depended on. If he can't answer your question, he can get the information for you.

Use your banker. Get his advice. He is your best guide in this money-making jungle.

$$ How Jeff B. Used Inside Bank Tips to Borrow $100,000 — No Strings Attached

I am going to let you in on a secret most bankers use, and you must learn to use it to your advantage.

To make money, *"Go where the money is."*

If your sink leaks, you get in touch with a plumber; if your car won't start, you call a mechanic. The same principle applies to making money. Seek out a good bank, savings and loan association, or the Small Business Administration. This is where the flow of money begins. You must learn how to use borrowed money (other people's money) on our road to riches. *To succeed, you must raise capital.*

Many people don't understand why a lending institution refuses to loan them money, while a next door neighbor can obtain a loan any time he desires. If they do get a loan, they find strings attached. Such people fail to understand that banks and lenders have to operate by certain principles just the same as any other business.

I would like to relate some experiences I have

had as a loan officer of a bank. The following are examples: (I have changed names to prevent embarrassment to anyone.)

Tom S. told me, "I will never bank here again", after he was refused a business loan, although I had explained to Tom that his business wasn't earning enough to meet expenses, much less assume a large loan payment.

Will J. lost his temper in my office, because he didn't know what kind of financing or how much financing he needed. A bank will hesitate to loan money if you have only a vague idea of why you need the money.

Knowledge of money facts would have saved these men the embarrassment of losing their tempers; but more important, such facts would have helped them borrow money at a time when their businesses needed it badly. I am going to explain a few inside bank tips you will need to know so you will never be caught in an embarrassing situation when you apply for money.

You will find four inside bank tips listed that enabled Jeff B. of Oklahoma City, to obtain a $100,000 loan to open a plant to manufacture mini-blinds. Have *all* the answers — because your ability to borrow money is just as important as your location, proper equipment, supplies or your employees. Before a bank or lending institution will loan money to you, they must have answers to the following questions:

1. *What sort of person are you? Is your credit sound? The character of a borrower comes first.*
2. *What are you going to use the money for? This determines the type of loan, short term or long term. If you were buying seasonal merchandise, you would want a short-term loan. If buying equipment or fixtures, you would ask for a long-term loan.*
3. *How do you plan to repay the loan? Is your*

business earning enough to justify the repayment schedule, or do you have another source of income?

4. Financial statements are a must. (Your bank has the forms.) Your bank wants to make loans to solvent businesses and wants to see you grow. When preparing your statement, make sure it is accurate. If you add a lot of "water," you will only drown later.

HOW TO KNOW THE KIND OF MONEY YOU NEED

What kind of money. When you set out to borrow for your new venture of existing business, you must know the kind of money you need. There are three kinds of money: short term, long term, and equity capital.

Short term money is just what it says, a short period of time — 30, 60 or 90 days repayment period. This kind of money is often used to build an inventory or accounts receivable, which can be repaid when it has served its purpose. Banks often grant this kind of loan on your credit rating or inventory.

Long Term Borrowing. This kind of loan enables you to obtain money you can repay over a long period of time, usually on installments. It can be broken down in two forms: (1) Intermediate — loan longer than one year, but less than five; (2) Long term — repaid over a period more than five years.

Remember this one point: Match your repayment schedule to the earnings of your business. The quicker you repay, the less interest you must pay.

Equity Capital. Don't ever confuse term borrowing with equity capital. *You don't have to repay equity capital.* It is money that you get by selling a part of your business. You take people into your business who are willing to bet you are going to be successful.

This is a good way to start a new enterprise, but a word of caution. Never sell control of your business.

You could wind up on the outside looking in on a profitable business you conceived and built.

SMALL BUSINESS ADMINISTRATION LOANS

If you exhaust all means for a loan, don't forget your rich uncle — *Uncle Sam*. The SBA's primary goal is to promote small businesses so that they can contribute to the economic growth of the country. At present, the SBA may guarantee up to 90% or $350,000, whichever is less, of a loan. However, the SBA will only consider making a direct loan when a guaranteed bank loan is not available.

Here is a little tip to save you time. You must first apply to a bank or private source for money before making application to the SBA. If you live in a city of over 200,000 population, you must apply at two banks, and you must be rejected, before they will consider your application.

We are going to give you a check list to study before making application to the SBA:

The SBA will not make loans:

1. *If you can obtain money elsewhere.*
2. *If the proceeds are to be used to pay debts.*
3. *If the loan allows speculation in property.*
4. *If your business is a non-profit organization.*
5. *If you plan to re-loan the money.*
6. *If you make a living from gambling.*
7. *If the loan is used to relocate for other than a sound business purpose.*

TIPS TO AID YOU

For a New Business:

1. Have a resume to show your experience and ability to manage your business.

2. Set out in detail the type of business you plan to establish.

3. Prepare an estimate of how much money is needed and how much you plan to put into the business.

4. Prepare a current financial statement.

5. List collateral to be used for security and its present market value.

6. Show a detailed projection of earnings for the first year.

For Established Business:

1. Show amount of money needed and purpose for which it will be used.

2. Prepare a current personal financial statement plus a balance sheet on your business.

3. List collateral to be used and its value.

4. Have a profit and loss statement for the previous year.

When you have all this available information, it shows the loan officer that you have done your homework, and your chances of obtaining a loan will be increased.

You must remember the SBA is a public agency which uses taxpayer's money — not a charity organization. But, you will find they are a great help in obtaining funds for a new or existing business.

HOW TO PAY YOURSELF FIRST — WITH INTEREST

On your road to dealing like a millionaire, you must start saving money. Make it a rule to pay yourself first.

When you begin to accumulate dollars to save, opening a savings account is a simple procedure. But, you should do a little shopping around before you decide where you are going to save your money. Not only could you get a higher interest return, but better service.

One study revealed a difference of 171% in yield between two interest paying systems, even though the interest rate in both cases was the same.

What is the interest rate? Rates differ in various sections of the country, and West coast lenders tend to pay more. The interest paid may vary from one lender to another, even between accounts in the same institutions.

The present Federal regulations allow commercial banks to pay up to 5% on passbook accounts; savings and loan companies and savings banks can pay up to 5½ %. However, the law doesn't say they must pay the maximum, so find out — it could be much lower.

Certificates of Deposit (CD's) are permitted to pay a higher rate. For example: A $1,000 CD may pay 7½ % if held for four years. It would be good if you checked with your bank for the minimum amount for the highest rate. Also, Federal regulations governing interest rates are subject to change. Keep close watch for any changes that will affect your personal savings.

Credit unions that have a Federal charter can pay dividends up to 7% on share accounts, and some state chartered credit unions can go even higher. A word to the wise — a credit union can't guarantee the dividend rate, and share accounts are available only to those qualified to join.

1. *How often is interest credited?* You know that the more often interest is credited, the better. A bank or lender may compound often or sometimes continually, but credit the interest less often. Interest can draw interest only after it has been credited to your

account. Naturally, after the interest has been credited, you can withdraw it if you wish.

2. *How is interest figured?* This is a technical question and has to do with the bookkeeping method. You may be hard pressed to get a straight answer.

Some banks pay interest on the lowest balance in your account during an interest period; others deduct your withdrawals from the balance you started with; some institutions debit withdrawals from the first deposit after your opening balance; others credit withdrawals against your recent deposit and some pay interest for all the actual number of days money remains in your account. The last day of deposit to day of withdrawal is found to be the best.

3. *When does interest earning take place?* Some banks will give a certain number of days grace during which you may make deposits or withdrawals without losing any interest. The more days you can get the better.

4. *Penalties to avoid.* If a savings account isn't used, some institutions may stop paying interest and may charge a "maintenance fee" which may run as much as $12 a year. To avoid an early closing charge, some banks require you to keep your account for a certain period of time.

Also, there is a Federal regulation that if a depositor withdraws savings from a time deposit, he must forfeit 90 days interest and the interest is reduced to a passbook level.

How many withdrawals can you make without a fee? Check this out. Some allow as many as you wish. Others have a charge.

To get all of the facts and figures may be difficult in some places because I have found most of the personnel do not know the answers. Don't give up. Start paying yourself first.

How long will your savings last?

This table shows how much you could withdraw each month from various amounts of savings before the funds would be depleted. The chart assumes the money is in an account earning interest at 5¼% from day of deposit to day of withdrawal, compounded daily.

amount on deposit	years of monthly withdrawals			
	5	10	15	20
$ 5,000	$ 95.11	$ 53.84	$ 40.41	$ 33.92
7,500	142.67	80.77	60.61	50.88
10,000	190.22	107.69	80.82	67.85
12,500	237.78	134.62	101.03	84.81
15,000	285.45	161.54	121.23	101.77
17,500	332.89	188.46	141.44	118.73
20,000	380.45	215.39	161.64	135.70
22,500	428.01	242.31	181.85	152.66
25,000	475.56	269.24	202.06	169.62
27,500	523.12	296.16	222.26	186.58
30,000	570.68	323.09	242.47	203.55
32,500	618.24	350.01	262.68	220.51
35,000	665.79	376.93	282.88	237.47
37,500	713.35	403.86	303.09	254.44
40,000	760.91	430.78	323.29	271.40
42,500	808.46	457.71	343.50	288.36
45,000	856.02	484.63	363.71	305.32
47,500	903.58	511.55	383.91	322.29
50,000	951.13	538.48	404.12	339.25

Enter amount of savings you have at present on another sheet of paper.

Enter amount you expect to have one year from today on the same sheet.

CHECK POINTS FOR
CHECKING ACCOUNTS

It is obvious that in order to operate a business you must have a checking account. Before you open an account, shop around for the best deal. If you have a business account, take a look around. You may wish to change.

1. Free checking accounts. There are two types of free checking accounts. One is completely free — no charge. The other is a modified plan. The free account is offered to special groups such as senior citizens, youth groups, etc., but I have seen ordinary "Joes" with one. "Ask and sometimes you may receive." If not, you can get the modified plan whereby you may be required to subscribe to other bank services to get free checking privileges, such as: keeping a savings account in the bank, use their bank credit cards or their overdraft loan feature on your checking account. You may be required to keep a minimum balance or make a sizeable initial deposit. They also may require a combination of services.

2. Regular checking accounts. The fees on this account are usually based on the balance and the activity in your checking account. If you keep a certain balance and don't exceed a number of items, you won't be charged anything. For example, if your balance is less than $200, there may be a service charge of $1.50 and you are allowed nine items a month. If you keep a balance of $200 to $299, you may pay no service charge and receive 10 free transactions; if over $300, you may receive 13 free items.

3. Special accounts. When you are unable to get a free checking account and write only a few checks, you may prefer this type of account. Under this plan, you don't maintain any required balance.

You are charged a fixed amount for each transaction and sometimes a small monthly charge.

Also, you will want to check and see how often they mail out their bank statements. Some mail each month and others, every other month.

4. *Analysis checking accounts.* Once your business account increases to the point that you keep large sums of money in your account, *this is the plan you need.*

You only pay a fixed charge for each transaction, plus a maintenance fee like a special account. However, you get a *bonus.* You earn credit on your balance which is deducted from your charges.

5. *Little things to find out.*

(a) How much do checks cost?

(b) What is an item? Some banks may view an item on each check or debit paid on your account each time you make a deposit or any check you cash at the bank.

(c) How are balances defined? If you must maintain a certain balance, does it spell out the exact amount, or do they use the average amount in your account during the month?

(d) Extra charges? Do they charge for stop-payment orders, overdrafts, statements issued at times other than regular dates?

Find out all you can. After all, it is your money and you can be sure they are going to use it to make money for the bank.

HOW TO WALK INTO ANY BANK AND GET THE MONEY YOU WANT FOR A NEW IDEA

Here is inside information that I learned while serving on the Board of Directors of an Oklahoma City bank. It works. Believe me, I have seen it happen many times.

For instance: You have a good idea for a business or service. If you really have a winner and need money, approach several banks. Not to borrow money, but ask if they know an investor who might be interested. You probably won't talk to over two V.P.'s before they ask to invest, or they are on the phone to a customer they know who likes to invest in risk ventures. Remember $10,000 — $30,000 is no money to an investor, and the bank takes no risk. You make your deal with the investor. Of course, the investor gets part of the action plus interest on his money, but you will always remember them as friends who put you on the road to dealing like a millionaire.

CHAPTER THREE

HOW TO DISCOVER MILLION-DOLLAR DEALS USING OTHER PEOPLE'S MONEY

In this chapter I am going to show you how to have more fun, more excitement, and make more money than you ever made in your life. All it is going to cost you is the printing of a few business cards and maybe later, your own personal letterheads with envelopes to match.

That is the total outlay of cash which is probably less than a twenty dollar bill — for you to start dealing like a millionaire — with other people's money.

HOW THREE SIMPLE BANKING
TERMS WILL PUT YOU IN THE
MILLION DOLLAR CLASS

Remember this one valuable secret used by all men who become millionaires — they know that different things have a different meaning to different people. For example: In every town there is an individual — you may know one yourself — who always drives a big car, wears the finest suits money can buy, and always has plenty of money to spend. You talk to him for ten minutes and find out he is working on a deal.

Do you recognize this man? Sure you do. Everyone in town has put a label on him — the "Wheeler Dealer."

I will now show you human nature — plus how to deal like a millionaire.

I have a friend, Ralph Henderson, a former bank director, who does exactly the same thing as our "wheeler dealer" friend. He drives a Cadillac, wears good clothes and has plenty of money; but he has a different label. He is known as a "business financial consultant" — three simple terms Ralph picked up while associated with the bank.

These three "magic" bank terms can put you in the million dollar class, playing with other people's money and never risking a cent of your own.

The reason is simple. The banking term "business financial consultant" makes you a third party in all money-making deals. When you find someone who has a proposition you hand him your business card with your name, address and telephone number, with the words "Business Financial Consultant" printed in fancy letters, and inform them you represent a third party.

There is a reason for this. It eliminates you from having to procure a financial statement to prove your net worth. Also, you won't have your credit investigated, and it gives you the first chance to get in with no money of your own.

But, that is not all. It is common practice in the financial and business world to have third parties represent people with large sums of money, or institutions who are looking for deals to increase their assets.

This is why the people you are offering these deals to are not suspicious when approached by a third party representing someone else — whose name is not revealed for obvious reasons.

These three magic terms printed on your business card will open doors to wheeling and dealing like a millionaire, in everything from ice cream wagons to jet aircraft. You will take over real estate, businesses, and acquire the luxuries of life you never dreamed of because of your limited finances.

HOW TO GET PEOPLE TO THRUST MONEY ON YOU

As I mentioned, the first thing you must do is to have some fancy business cards printed with the three magic bank terms on them and with your name, address and telephone number. With these in your pocket, you are ready to deal like a millionaire — with other people's money.

First, go to your banker, then to realtors, lawyers, CPA's, and anyone you know who engages in money-making deals.

You simply present your card, and tell them you represent a wealthy party who is interested in a good financial proposition. Explain that if anything comes to their attention that your client or clients will give it careful consideration. Tell them they should call you the moment anything looks good.

What happens? They begin to spread the word around that you are representing someone with a large bank account who wishes to invest in a good proposition.

Often, in a matter of hours, people with deals will start ringing your telephone.

The people you contacted and left your business cards with will soon call and tell you what propositions they have located.

You now request full details, what is offered, the asking price, terms and conditions, and so forth.

Have them send all this to you in the form of a written proposal — which you in turn, can sit down and analyze, to see if there is any potential in it.

Here I might mention that when it is learned that you are representing people with funds to invest, people you never heard of will begin to seek you out to invest their money. They will literally *thrust money* on you for you to invest for them, for handsome fees — There is a lot of idle money just sitting in banks, waiting for a business financial consultant like yourself.

But that is not all — *deals, deals, deals* — you will be swamped with deals of all kinds for you to check out. You get first chance at all the lucrative ones.

Remember this, you have no money to invest, and all the good deals require some money. What is your next step?

HOW TO USE YOUR BANKER
TO FLUSH OUT
MILLION-DOLLAR DEALS

If, while checking into your most lucrative deals, you find one you would like to get in on — You do a turn-around and start looking for investors or a client.

Here is where your banker can help you. Let me say right here that when you are cultivating the friendship of a banker, don't waste time on a third vice president. Get to know the president, or at least a senior vice president. These men are trained to loan money, or where to find money, and they enjoy their work, especially if they can figure out a way to make a little side money and not violate any banking laws.

As I mentioned, you have found a deal. For example: Say the CPA you left your card with has presented you with a proposition to acquire a medical building. After you find that it is a good deal, you start presenting the deal to lending agencies. You will get turned down a few times, but you will find one who will lend a certain percentage of the funds to acquire or refinance the building.

Now, here is where your banker can help you to deal like a millionaire.

Show him you have a tentative loan amount from a lender, and explain you need an investor to pick up the difference, or use his financial statement for a percentage of the business.

Your banker should have a friend in mind. If not, you can suggest that he mention your proposition at the next Board of Directors meeting, because 99% of these board members have risk capital to invest, or they have a friend or relative just waiting for a good deal to come along.

Here is a secret all millionaires know — people invest for one reason only — money.

After your banker friend has spread the word around, a member of the Board or some other investor he has flushed out contacts you.

At this point, you lay out the complete plan showing that you can acquire the medical building. Show him the cash flow, which shows a handsome profit after all expenses and taxes. You now begin to deal like a millionaire. Tell your investor you can refinance the building with a new loan, with no cash involved, if he is financially strong enough, and you will give him, say, 70% of the deal, just for the use of his name. (You may have to give 80-90% to get him to accept the deal without your having to put up any money.)

You have an excellent chance to own an interest in a medical building. All you have done is a little leg work, asked a few questions, and put your banker to work flushing out deals and investors.

You may say that this kind of dealing is unusual — that is true — but it works.

You must keep in mind when you are dealing, that the information you have is worth a lot of money. When the person you are dealing with doesn't have it, all you do is set the value and never sell it cheap or give it away free.

Please remember that you aren't going to cash in on every proposition that comes to you. You are going to lose the majority because your investor won't go for the deal. And don't be surprised if they steal the deal from you. But, persistence pays off. One day, you will close a deal that is going to make you a lot of money.

So, that is why you can afford to make mistakes and lose all kinds of different deals. You haven't lost anything but time, but you are getting an education that money can't buy. You are acquiring the touch to understand how millionaires deal, and one day you will find you are making deals you never dreamed of before you became a Business Financial Consultant.

Sooner or later, your income is going to sky-rocket beyond your wildest dreams.

HOW TO BUILD A
NETWORK OF INFORMANTS
WORTH A MILLION DOLLARS
TO YOU

The real key to dealing like a millionaire is getting people to help you find investors or finance money-making deals. To do this you need a network of informants.

You must build a friendship with your local banker, and don't overlook your doctor. Doctors are always looking for a place to invest money. Bookkeepers know their clients assets. Real estate salesmen enjoy making extra money on the side. Just take out your notebook and start making a list of people who can send deals your way. You will be surprised just how many you can list.

The best way to get their attention and make them your "informants" is to give them a piece of the action on the deals you complete with their help. If they don't want part of the deal, set up a fee arrangement, or give them a few percentage points; anything to get them to swing the deals your way.

Participation is the key that will build a network of informants that could be worth a million dollars to you.

But please remember, if you try to keep the whole pie for yourself you will lose many valuable contracts. You will still make a few deals, but you will find many people will turn a deaf ear to your propositions.

Spread the money around. Make everybody feel like they are a millionaire and the sky is the limit to the vast sums of money you can promote.

$$ How Dale G. Picked up $50,000 Yearly Income — Without any Cash

There is money everywhere, just waiting for someone to pick it up. Take the case of Dale G., a bright young man who was a West Texan school teacher. A friend (an Informant) had referred him to a section of land that was planted as a wheat crop. There was also over $100,000 worth of machinery involved.

He got into the deal with no cash up front —
with the provision that he could sell the farm machinery over the year and apply the proceeds to the
cost of the land — which reduced his debt and increased his equity in the land.

But, that is not all. He also received the income
when the wheat crop was harvested. (He subcon-
tracted the cutting of the crop to a neighbor for the
next year's seed crop. There was still no outlay of
cash.) The second year he began to enjoy over
$50,000 a year income. All he did was work up a
deal, like a millionaire, and present it.

There are dozens of opportunities to take over
businesses on that same basis, where there is an excess of equipment or goods that can be sold with the
proceeds applied to the cost of purchase.

Your banker should be able to put you onto a
good deal. They may have a business loan in default
that they would be glad to give you. Ask and you
shall receive.

One of the finest examples of dealing without
any cash, is Joe M., a young man who was out of work
and wanted to own a gas station during the gas short-
age. This would seem to be the least likely time to
start — but not for this young entrepreneur.

Joe M. got on the phone and began to hunt for
gasoline for his station. At first, all he found was a
lot of people wanting gas. Then Joe began to call
himself an "oil company", and discovered there
were people with gas to sell. So, he began to act as
a middleman and would match buyer with seller —
for a fee.

One day Joe came up with a half million dollar
deal, but he didn't have the money and the banks
wouldn't advance him any cash. So, what did he do?
Joe approached the buyer and asked him if he would
guarantee the deal. The buyer, happy to get gas,
hopped on Joe's deal. Armed with this information,
Joe, without any cash of his own, netted over

$1,000,000 in four months by matching buyers and sellers of gasoline.

This should give you a bright idea. If something is in short supply, with just a little leg work you can find a source who is willing to sell. Then, you can find a willing buyer at almost any price, and you take your percentage off the top.

$$ How to Invest Nothing and Turn a Profit While Doing It — Gus G's and Ralph B's Stories

Here is a classic story I read in the Wall Street Journal. This story is about a man named Gus G., who believed cash was overrated. He said "anyone who says you have to have it to make it, doesn't know what he is talking about".

Gus was a school teacher by profession, who used a little savvy and borrowed money to become rich. He has ownership of several banks and buildings, one of which is the Tropicana Hotel in Las Vegas.

It all started in his local bank when he asked the bank how much they would loan on a 160-apartment complex in a nearby development.

The bank made an appraisal that was $200,000 in excess of what Gus knew he could purchase it for — the total was 1.8 million dollars. Gus closed the deal, became the owner of an apartment complex and had $200,000 for walking around money. He invested no money of his own. All he did was ask a bank to make a simple appraisal on a piece of property.

In a similar deal, Ralph B., of Houston, Texas, found a 2.6 million dollar shopping center that had been for sale almost a year. The reason it hadn't sold was that it didn't produce enough income from leases to encourage anyone to put up 2.6 million dollars.

After expenses, taxes and insurance, the net

profit was hardly $27,000, or 1% of capital invested, not a good deal for an investor.

So, Ralph got the details on the shopping center, went to a savings and loan, and asked if they would appraise and give him the amount they would loan on the property.

They made the appraisal, and came up with a figure of 2.1 million dollars, without additional collateral. He took the proposition to the owners and offered the 2.1 million for the center if they would pay all the loan costs on the new loan, plus any penalty for paying off the existing loan. They were eager to sell and the deal was closed. The net results were that Ralph became the owner of a 2.6 million dollar shopping center, and got $27,000 income from the property.

From a banker's standpoint, this was the worst investment a man could make — only 1% return on a 2.1 million dollar investment. But, from Ralph's viewpoint, he was dealing like a millionaire and getting rich on borrowed money. And, to him, it was one of the best deals he ever made.

Once you grasp the idea that you are not interested in great return on your investment, but just a return, then you can make all kinds of deals. And that is how you can invest nothing and turn a profit while doing it.

Even if the deal falls through, you have lost nothing but time. It's just the same as if you were fishing or golfing. There is one difference: One strike and you are rich.

HOW TO FORM YOUR OWN INVESTMENT GROUP — YOU GET MOST OF THE ACTION FREE

As I mentioned, when the word gets around and you build a reputation for knowing how to make money, you will be approached by people in all types of businesses who have money to invest and will almost insist that you show them how to make money.

Now, you begin to make a list of investors you believe in. Pool their money to form "XYZ Investment Group".

Explain that in numbers there is strength and they can all profit from any acquired deals that you put together.

Form a small corporation if you wish, but as the manager, you are entitled to a salary plus a piece of the action.

There are more people around with money looking for an aggressive person who can dig up investment deals than you ever thought there would be. Take advantage of this golden opportunity to form your own investment group, while you get a salary, plus a piece of the action — free.

The opportunities to deal like a millionaire are everywhere. It is just a simple matter of putting your plan into action. Tell everyone you meet that you have clients with money to invest. Tell everyone you meet that you have propositions for people who have money to invest.

I know this takes a lot of nerve, but remember, Mr. Conrad Hilton bought his first hotel when he was flat broke — on nerve and borrowed money. And, as long as you are not investing any of your own money, the risk is small.

After a couple of deals, when you get the feel of putting the deals together, you will begin to see profits that you never knew existed. And, in addition to that, you will have the full confidence that you can deal like a millionaire with other people's money.

CHAPTER FOUR

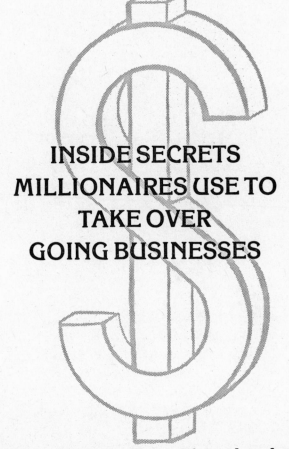

INSIDE SECRETS MILLIONAIRES USE TO TAKE OVER GOING BUSINESSES

A man can work all his life and end up with nothing to show for it except social security or a small pension. He may be forced to find extra work just to pay his bills. Isn't that reason enough to go into business for yourself?

It is not a coincidence that millionaires are their own bosses. They are the men who make their own future, which brings us to inside secrets millionaires use to take over going businesses. And, it brings up the question, "Should I run the risk of being my own boss, or should I strive to be a manager of someone else's company?"

These are questions you must answer someday. As I mentioned, to deal like a millionaire, you must take risks. But, whoever you are, you can become wealthy.

Study, understand and apply the principles contained in this chapter if you really want to take over a going business. Here is the starting point.

HOW TO DEAL ON
PROPERTIES — NOT SCHEMES

Risk is the key element of life. Every morning when we get up, there is the risk that we could die before sundown. Knowing this, we take precautions or exercise good judgment to reduce the odds. We obey traffic rules and watch our health, in short, we do everything we can to improve our chances of staying alive.

When we take a risk, it is an intelligent risk based on information and experience, which leads us to a normal and useful life. In the *art of dealing on properties*, we must do the same thing — take only intelligent risks. And remember, as I mentioned in Chapter 2, the difference between a gambler and a speculator in property is intelligent risk.

A gambler bets on a hunch or a friendly tip. The speculator also bets, but he will weigh the facts at hand and judge his returns against odds. Then he will decide if he wants to risk his money. The successful real estate speculator puts his money up only when the *odds are in his favor.*

In dealing like a millionaire, we must take risks in speculating and investments, and I don't believe any banker can tell you the difference. I have seen what seemed a sound investment turn into a speculation overnight, and vice versa. Many a speculation has turned into a profitable investment. Also, sudden turns of events have often put company executives in bad trouble with their Board of Directors.

For instance, one executive I know invested several thousand dollars in a cattle feed lot operation in Colorado. Cattle prices were high, and on paper it looked like a sound investment. But, one morning when our friend woke up, the bottom had fallen out of the cattle market and his company faced a huge loss. The Board of Directors demoted our executive for bad judgment. However, if the market had gone up and the company had made a fortune, they would have labeled our friend a genius.

There is one fact that escapes many entrepreneurs: everyone responsible for money is a trustee. They should know that "risk and safety" sometimes look like twins, and the best of promoters can't tell them apart. That is why to deal like a millionaire, we must take risks. And if there is a safe speculation, it would have to be property, not some scheme yet unborn.

In my lifetime as a banker, I have never seen any property that wasn't worth something — regardless of how old or beat up it was. It has a value and can be sold — there is a buyer somewhere for anything if we just look long enough.

Recently, a man, whose name I won't mention, came to me for a loan for a scheme — one that couldn't fail. His neighbor had invested — it was a pyramid game on vitamins — and he wanted in. Why? Because he was dealing with a hope that his investment would triple overnight. Sorry to say, he lost his money. Later, we met at a luncheon, and he told me he had charged his loss to education.

If you are going to invest in schemes, make sure you can afford it. The failure rate runs high — not one in fifty is successful.

Put your money in properties — it can't vanish

into thin air. With a good promotion any property can be turned into a profit. But, that is not all, property appreciates or depreciates, regardless of the owner. Also, the owner of properties isn't as easily fooled or talked out of his money. If you must speculate, start in property.

A MILLIONAIRE'S SECRET — HOW YOU CAN PICK UP PROPERTIES — NEVER INVESTING OVER $1.00 OF YOUR OWN MONEY

The idea is to invest no cash and to turn a nice profit out of doing it. Here is why this plan works. You are not interested in a percent return on investment; you are simply interested in a profit. Since you have nothing invested, if the deal goes sour, you are out nothing.

Step #1: Here is an example of how Richard K., a real estate salesman, makes the $1.00 option plan work:

You find a good piece of land or a commercial lot — one you can develop using our plan. Then, you go to the owner and ask him for a 90-day option on the property at a quoted price. Explain you have a third party interested and you have to present the deal to them. The property would have to be under your control for 90 days to work out the deal. The owner, with nothing to lose, would gladly give you an option to sell at his price. The option agreement is signed and you give him $1.00 for the option consideration.

Step #2: You go to an architect and have him draw up a floor plan of a small building (you get the architect to do this on the speculation of doing the complete job). Now, find someone who would like to exchange their lease for occupation of a building with *their name* on it.

Step #3: For instance, you contact Smith & Son

Insurance Co. and offer to build them a complete office building and call it The Smith & Sons Building. Also, the rent just might be less than they are paying at present. Sooner or later, you are going to find someone. Have them sign an "Intent to Lease Contract", stating how much per square foot they will pay.

Step #4: You now have the cost of land, cost of building, and lease agreement. You now take your package to an aggressive savings and loan company, and get 100% financing. The income from the lease pays loan payments, insurance, taxes and upkeep — and leaves a profit for yourself. You have never been out any pocket money, except your $1.00 option payment.

One or two deals a year and you could become a millionaire over the years.

Incidentally, the $1.00 option can work with many angles. Wayne D., of Lincoln, Nebraska, used the plan with farm tractors. He would approach a farmer to buy his tractor at a quoted price and get a 30 day option to pay off. He would soon have four or five tractors on option, and would then run a classified ad in the local paper saying "Tractor for Sale." He would show his tractors and would sell at least two or three a month.

Try a few simple transactions, then move into the big money. You have nothing to lose, except a $1.00 option. There is an old saying "Nothing Ventured — Nothing Gained," proven true a million times in the past hundred years.

$$ How George D., Working with His Banker, Receives $800.00 per Month — From a Business not His Own

If you can locate a business that looks like it is hopelessly in debt, and the creditors are getting worried about a voluntary bankruptcy, you might want to try the same plan used by George D., a loan company employee who was familiar with consolidating debts of customers and pro-rating debts of small businesses.

Work with your banker. He may have a business on the books in this situation. If he doesn't, the next step is to locate one, by asking him to make inquiries of his fellow banker friends.

Once you have found a business in this overloaded debt situation, your first step is to visit the current owner.

Explain to him that his business is going down the drain with the present debt load, and no one would ever consider buying it until the indebtedness is reduced. However, you have a plan that will see that he gets something for his business, rather than allowing his creditors to force him out of business. If he wants to give your plan a try, your next step is to contact his creditors.

Have the owner give you a list of all his creditors and the total debts of each. And, in addition, have him figure out the total monthly income of the business.

For example: Lets say the business income per month is $1,000 after operating expenses, plus a fee each month for yourself. (George D. asked $200 a week or $800 a month for his services.)

Now, working with your banker, you contact all the creditors and tell them you have made arrangements with the bank to put in trust or escrow, $1,000 each month, and that they will receive payment on a pro-rated basis on the percent debt owed, provided they agree to settle for 50¢ on the dollar. All future business would be on a cash basis.

Why will the creditors agree to settle their accounts for 50¢ on the dollar? Simple arithmetic: 50¢ is greater than 10¢ or zero. They know if the business goes bankrupt, they may get nothing, and if they did, it could take months to collect. With your paln they have a chance to recover something on a bad debt. Of course, you will have to do a good sales job to make the plan work.

But, that is not all, you now begin to deal like a millionaire and take over the business. You have satisfied the creditors — and the indebtedness has been reduced 50%. You go to the owner and tell him you wish to buy his business and you will assume all liability, freeing him from the huge debt load. You will pay him out of the business, as soon as the present debts have been liquidated.

How much you pay for the business will depend on how anxious he wants out and what the business is worth. If he doesn't sell, you still have a monthly income for your services of setting up the Debt Pro-Rate Plan. A couple of plans a year could put you on the road to riches.

HOW A CHAPTER 10
BANKRUPTCY PUTS DOLLARS
IN YOUR POCKET

You may find that there are several creditors who refuse to go along with your Pro-Rate Plan. However, you can still take over the business if the present owner will agree to forming a corporation.

You may find an attorney who will form the corporation for a certain number of shares, but once the corporation is formed, have your attorney file a Chapter 10 Bankruptcy. This allows the business to keep operating. But that is not all. The court now works out a pro-rate payment schedule for the creditors — which may be less money than you offered in your plan. Also, the creditor can no longer contact the owner, and in addition, the creditors have to take the court settlement whether they like it or not.

The corporation also limits your personal liability while the Chapter 10 Bankruptcy puts dollars in your pocket.

THE CLOSELY GUARDED SECRET OF "THE BUST OUT SYSTEM" WILL GET YOU MILLION DOLLAR RESULTS

We learned of this system from Alex F., a customer of the bank. He had requested a loan to replace the inventory of a clothing store he had recently purchased.

From the information gathered, here is how it works:

You find a business that is overstocked on merchandise and where the owner has exhausted his credit and is ready to sell. You offer to buy with a small down payment, and the owner takes a promissory note for the inventory on easy monthly payments.

The day you take over the business, you make arrangements for an "Emergency Cash Sale," running ads in local papers with a big splash. Then, you sell off the merchandise at a reduced price, say 50%, and use the proceeds of the sale to repay any outstanding debts.

If you made a good deal with the owner on the purchase of the inventory, you can still make a good profit on your "Bust Out Sale."

After the sale, approach your banker, as Alex F. did, for a loan to replace your inventory. Also, many suppliers will be eager to extend you credit. Of course, you must have some knowledge of the type of business you purchase. Please remember, the Bust Out System works, and could produce million dollar results for you.

THE MAGIC ART OF
CONVERTING OTHERS TO
SELL ON YOUR TERMS

Credit is the oil that keeps the free enterprise system's wheels turning. Credit has enabled our Capitalist system to have the highest living standard in the world, but that is not all. It can help us convert others to sell their business to you on your terms.

Most businessmen don't understand the principle of factoring. A factor is a person who puts up cash with accounts receivable as security, and collects the accounts at a discount.

The large factoring companies such as banks, won't handle small businesses. If they did, they would want to hold out too much for uncollectable accounts. This leaves the field wide open for you. All you need to do is find a company that has a high volume of credit business and limited capital.

Here is an opportunity to use your banker again. He may have some small company he would like to turn over to a private factor.

When you have located a company with a volume of credit business and limited capital, you have an excellent prospect for a takeover.

Now, you find an individual who has money to loan. Your banker can tell you who has idle money and who is looking for a chance to make 10% or more on this money. If unable to find one through your banker, run a few ads in your local newspaper. Once you have located an investor, you work with his banker to set up a factoring system that will pay them a handsome return, plus a set sum for you.

If you set up a 10% discount for 30-60 day accounts, that is approximately 60% to 120% per year return on investment capital.

In a short time you own all the accounts receivable — Now, you have leverage to purchase the business on your terms and pay for it out of the money received from your service as the factoring agent.

But please remember, you must collect accounts quickly and increase the credit business. It is the percentage return on capital invested that accounts for the high profits. If accounts are allowed to ride past due dates — you will end up just another collection agency.

HOW YOUR BANK AND ANOTHER MAN'S EQUIPMENT CAN MAKE YOU RICH ON BORROWED MONEY

Ken B. was an apprentice printer for a daily newspaper, barely making ends meet. In fact, at one time, the bank loaned him $600 to buy a '65 Ford to get back and forth to his job. Today, he owns his own print shop and is doing a $50,000 a year business.

Ken was not satisfied with his job and began to look for a print shop for sale. He located one in the "Business for Sale" section in the newspaper ads where he worked. He made arrangements to purchase it, with less than $100 in the bank.

You can do the same. Here is how this take over plan works:

You find a business for sale that has a lot of equipment and merchandise that is free and clear. If you see a way you can operate it with your experience to make a profit, this would be an opportunity to purchase, using the equipment or machinery as collateral for a loan at your bank.

First, you must arrive at a fair market value of the equipment. Not the owner's value, because he may place a lot of sentimental value on it — especially if he is going to retire.

The best way to find out the value is to get a couple of bids, as if you were going to sell it. Then you can arrive at a fair value for you and for the owner.

Now, here comes the part that will test your skill as a negotiator. Explain that you wish to use his equipment for collateral at your bank, to obtain a loan to buy the business, and you will need a "Bill of Sale", showing that you own the equipment free and clear.

If he balks, just tell him that without the equipment there is no way you can obtain financing. If he wants to sell, he will be glad to work with you and your banker.

When he agrees, take an inventory list to your banker and see how much capital you can raise.

If unable to get the amount you need, maybe the owner will carry a second mortgage with reasonable terms if you offer him a good rate of interest. As we mentioned, your bank and another man's equipment can make you rich on borrowed money.

HOW TO USE THE "DOUBLE LOAN PLAN" TO PICK UP A PROFITABLE BUSINESS FOR YOURSELF

When you offer to write a man a check for his business, it is amazing how quickly you can arrive at a selling price far below the asking price.

This plan works only if you have some borrowing power on your own signature at your bank. In fact, you should approach your banker and find out how much you can borrow on just your financial statement. Then you will know in advance how much you can write a check for, when you find a business you wish to buy.

This plan requires that you have established credit at two banks. For instance, you find a small business that you can buy for $6,000 cash. You write the man a check (make sure your bank will honor it), then you set up a $6,000 loan with payments of $300 per month. But, you may find the payments are too high for the income generated from your business.

Then, you go to your second bank or lender, and borrow $3,600 at $155 per month — and pay your first loan a year in advance with the $3600. You then resume the $155 a month payment on the second loan. At the end of the year, you simply consolidate the two loans into one. And, by this time, with good management, your business should be booming, and not only service the consolidated loan, but pay you a handsome profit.

HOW TO DEAL LIKE A MILLIONAIRE AND GAIN CONTROL OF A COMPETITOR'S BUSINESS — WITH NO CASH OF YOUR OWN

In the world of big corporations, when they gobble up a smaller competitor, they call it a merger. But that's not all. Often, large mergers must be approved by the government, to discourage price fixing, but with small businesses, it is simply called an acquisition. Regardless of what it is called, you have absorbed your competitor and use his manpower and resources to increase your own profits. It is good business and it is done every day.

The idea is to find a small competitor that is financially sound but struggling for business. You can offer a large share of your business for controlling interest. It may call for some skilled bargaining to get them to throw in with you. You would probably want to form a corporation with the number of shares based on the volume of business produced. This way, you control the business and have taken over your competitor with no outlay of cash of your own.

It can work — some are doing it every day.

"To venture is to risk anxiety, but not to venture is to lose yourself," said the philosopher Kierkegaard — Security is an elusive goal; to obtain it, you must take risks and deal like a millionaire.

CHAPTER FIVE

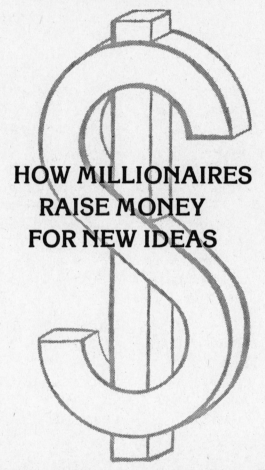

HOW MILLIONAIRES
RAISE MONEY
FOR NEW IDEAS

Let's say you have a new idea that will replace
the hula hoop or a franchise that McDonald's would
envy. There's only one hurdle — you don't have the
money to get your idea off the ground.

Your banker has refused you a business loan
and the small loan companies will advance only
$300.00, which wouldn't even buy a good used ice
box.

Don't give up. Any person who wishes to deal
like a millionaire can find the money for a good idea.

Remember, there are more people with money looking for a good investment than there are good business ideas available.

It is reported that over a quarter of a billion dollars of risk capital went begging last year for lack of
good ideas and business deals.

You may think that with this kind of money available, only large corporations have access to risk
capital funds — wrong. Many a risk capital investor
will look at your proposition, even if its only a $5,000
deal. This could be just the amount you need to put
your idea on the way to the moon.

But, please remember this. The risk investor
looks at his money as working capital, not as a risk.
They like to see the potential of a business or idea.
Large returns on a successful venture mean profits
for them.

Before you grab the telephone and start calling
risk capital investors, there are a few things you
should know:

*First: A venture capitalist expects a good return
on his invested capital — often a minimum of 25%.
So be prepared to pay. But, if you build a good solid
business that pays you a handsome profit in the years
ahead, you made a good deal. Count your investor as
a friend. After all, if you could get a better deal from
your banker, you would be sitting across from his
desk and not looking for risk capital.*

*Second: Be frank with your investor — if you
think it will take a year to turn a profit, tell him. Don't
make promises you can't keep.*

*Third: Never relinquish control of your business
or idea. You could wind up on the outside looking in
on a business you conceived.*

*Fourth: Here is a pointer that should never be
overlooked: Decide in advance what the repayment
terms are. When in doubt, have your attorney draw
up an agreement. Or, if your risk investor furnishes a*

contract, have your attorney examine it. It could be money well spent.

$$ How William D. Picked Up $40,000 Risk Capital With An Investment of $8.00

William D. had exceeded his credit limit at his local bank. He was unable to tap friends or relatives for a loan to promote a new insulation service for existing homes. He did what any resourceful entrepreneur would — he started thinking of ways to raise the money.

Why not run an ad in a daily newspaper? He did this for an $8.00 ad in the Business Opportunity section. William received an offer to put up the $40,000 for a 33-1/3% share of the business — he accepted. Today, has a booming business in home insulation.

Hard to believe? Not really. I ran a test ad in a national publication asking to borrow $100,000, and received 22 inquiries.

I am sure that at least one would have been a bona fide offer!

There are a few simple rules to follow in your search for risk capital via the newspaper:

First: State the amount of money you wish to borrow — If you only say you need "venture capital", many investors will pass you by.

Second: Let your prospective investor know what he can expect in return for his money. Do you wish to share part ownership of your business or a percent of profits? Or, do you prefer a straight interest rate? All these points are negotiable.

Third: State your idea or kind of business venture. This will serve to eliminate those not interested in your kind of proposition. It will save time and a lot of unnecessary correspondence.

Here is an ad, similar to the one that produced results for William D.

WANTED — $40,000.00 — New Home Insulation Company now being formed — Potential 50% return on invested capital. Minimum risk. Will furnish references and details to qualified investors. Write Box 103-X.

Never include your telephone number, because you will need a full time secretary to handle calls of promoters trying to get information on your deal so they can set up shop for themselves.

Please remember, you only need one investor. So, take your time in answering replies. Try to separate the wheat from the chaff. Keep your ad brief. Don't try to con your investor with long flowery phrases like "no other deal like this," or "double your money in 10 days." You only defeat your purpose. These investors didn't get surplus cash by falling for schemes.

Now, you have your ad written. Which paper should you use? If you are looking for someone to share ownership in the business, or an active partner, I suggest that you stay with your local newspaper. You never know who in your community might be looking for a deal.

But, if you are seeking a large sum, the Sunday papers of large metropolitan areas are the best. The risk investors pour over these ads looking for good investments.

If you need a million or more, you should use the financial publications that cover the United States.

Before spending any money on an ad, go to a newstand and purchase papers from various states. Look over the ads, especially the Wall Street Journal. You will find one section in the classifieds devoted to "Venture Capital." You will find all sizes and types.

Find the size you think will fit your purpose, then write your ad and place it in publications that you think will get the best results. Place the ad for a one-time run as a test. You should wait, but not for long. Shortly, your mail box will be filled with requests seeking information.

As I mentioned, you need only one investor, but you need to strike quickly, before your potential investor cools off. Answer every inquiry.

If they request your telephone number, give it, but heed one word of caution — don't explain your proposition over the telephone. Try to set up an appointment. Don't forget you have the money-making idea. So, deal like a millionaire, not like a beggar asking for dimes.

If they are genuinely interested in your proposition, they will be glad to see you. I recently had a risk investor offer to charter a plane for me to Pittsburgh. These men have money. But, that's not all. They are seeking opportunities to increase their wealth.

Don't show your hand by telephone or letter, only by appointment. You have everything to gain.

HOW TO SPOT A RISK
CAPITAL INVESTOR EAGER
TO LEND YOU MONEY

You don't have to be a banker to spot a risk capital investor, but you do need to know why he is in the business. Then you are in a better position to negotiate terms.

The man who is willing to put his money in a risk venture is a product of our income tax laws. He is searching for ways to keep his money, and at the same time, to increase the surplus funds he now owns.

For example, I have a friend, Cliff A., a real estate broker, whose personal income from various investments has placed him in the 50% tax bracket under the present tax laws. In other words, out of every dollar he earns, 50¢ goes to Uncle Sam and he gets to keep 50¢ for himself. So, it is natural for him to look for ways to keep part of the 50¢ from going to the Internal Revenue Service.

All risk investors are in the same boat. He can invest $100,000 in a risk venture, and if he loses all, he can deduct the loss on his tax return, and the government shares in half the loss, or $50,000.

But, that is not all, if his $100,000 makes him a $100,000 profit, and he is taxed at his regular rate of 50%, he makes $50,000. You see, our present tax laws (subject to change) created the risk investor, by paying for the majority of losses and letting him keep the biggest share of the profits.

You should be glad he exists as you "deal" like a millionaire and get rich on borrowed money. *His money works for you* just the same as your local bank's does. It is all printed on the same press.

That is why, with this background on risk investors, you should be able to spot one who is eager to lend you money.

Take a pencil and start thinking of people you know who are in this tax situation. For instance, your doctor. The next time you are in his office for a check up, let him know you have a proposition that can save him tax dollars, and at the same time increase his earnings. Don't overlook your neighbor who recently inherited a fortune, you can be sure he needs someone to invest his money. Your local storekeeper may be in the market to invest. You can make a long list. Contact them — The law of averages is working in your favor.

Another point in your favor is the tax deadline. An investor must hurry to find investments before he sends the majority of his income to his nearest "relative" — Uncle Sam.

Keep a sharp eye out. You will spot a risk investor who is eager to lend you money.

HOW TO SET UP A
FOOLPROOF INTERVIEW
WITH YOUR INVESTOR

First — Have you sold yourself on believing that your idea is a profitable venture, and not wishful day dreaming? — Have you done your homework and are you well prepared to meet your potential investor? Failure to prepare has left many a man with a good proposition without funds simply because he couldn't answer questions to the satisfaction of his risk investor.

Remember this one point — They aren't dumb individuals. If they don't know much about the field of business you are presenting, they can pick up the telephone, and in a few minutes, they will have information from an expert. So, don't try to con your prospect. Be honest, and above all, be prepared.

When you arrange your first interview, have enough time to develop your ideas. That's not all, because you are not going to lay out your complete plan at your first meeting — This is only a "get acquainted" meeting. Your investor learns the outline of your plan, and you find out if he is the principal party to deal with, or if he has others involved that he must consult before he can close the deal.

When you make your presentation, use an old trick of the pros to get the advantage — *Stand up while talking.* You will impress and convince your potential investor better than remaining seated.

Have you ever noticed that when you are seated, and someone else is standing, it puts you at a disadvantage. When you get excited about a subject and wish to make points — you should always get out of your chair to fire your best shot. Every person who wishes to "deal" like a millionaire will politely decline a seat when he is seeking to convince another person that his way or his idea is the only way to get rich. It works like electricity. You, standing, are the *positive* current; the person seated, the *negative*.

So, that is why, when you make your first call on your prospective investor, you wish to gain his confidence in you and your ability to carry out your money-making program. Talk straight from the shoulder, because you are trying to convince him your proposition is as attractive to him as it is to yourself.

Make your points clear. Prove that your proposition isn't the "run of the mill" business idea. Place your plan quickly before him and let him know that your time is valuable. In addition, you will be able to find out if he is interested in your proposition early in the interview. If he is enthusiastic about your program, then arrangements can be made for another meeting, where details can be worked out and he can review your plans, with all facts and figures, at his convenience.

Now, a very important point. When making arrangements for your next meeting, try to set it up in your own office. In closing a deal, the man in whose office the transaction takes place has the best advantage.

If you meet in a motel room or at an uninvolved person's office, you are on even ground — neither one has the advantage.

That is why professional men — bankers, lawyers, buyers — all have private offices for their clients to come to. They know this one great secret — "men fight best on their own home ground".

Try to set up your second meeting with your risk investor at your own place of business.

At your next meeting, take along your attorney. He could save you hundreds of dollars in later legal fees, wasted in trying to unravel the small print in a contract that you signed without the full knowledge of its contents

Also, with your attorney present, they are less likely to try to steal your idea.

HOW TO HIRE YOUR ATTORNEY FULL TIME WITH NO FEE

Hiring an attorney is an expensive proposition — but they are a must when legal contracts are involved.

We must remember that time is money to an attorney. You can make a deal like Ron F., who traded a percentage of his business for the time of his attorney.

There are attorneys who like speculative business — especially when all they have invested is time. When he has a share in your business, he makes sure you are protected legally in your venture, and you get the best side of the deal because he has an interest at stake.

For an added incentive, promise him that when the company is showing a profit, he gets to handle all company business on a fee basis.

One point of *advice* about attorneys. Don't take *their* advice on business matters. Attorneys, by their profession, spend most of their time with people or businesses that are in trouble. They are first trained in law, and second in business.

If you wish advice on your business, get it from your banker or fellow businessman. It's worth ten times the advice from your attorney.

Use your attorney as a reference. Let him draw up all your legal papers and let him keep you out of trouble. That's his business. Ask his advice on legal matters, never on the operation of your business.

Please remember that the best attorney wins the case. So, that is why you should have an attorney accompany you on your second interview with a prospective risk investor.

HELPING YOURSELF —
PROTECTING YOUR INTERESTS

Often when you are dealing like a millionaire and promoting your deals, you can over-sell yourself on the deal to the point that you become greedy — even before it gets off the ground. This creates a problem on how much interest in the business you should retain for yourself. There is usually one first question asked by a speculator. What is in it for me?

You should have what percentage you plan to retain in mind, and determine whether it is negotiable, in case your investor becomes hard-nosed about controlling interest. If you are broke, with no money to invest, try to retain at least 50%. If you relinquish 51%, you lose control of your business. And, in addition, don't overlook the fact that you have spent time putting the deal together. You should be reimbursed by the company, even at a later date when you are showing a profit.

Your salary as manager should be set at a reasonable level, with a cost-of-living increase as the business prospers. Be fair and your investor will go overboard to help put your idea on a paying basis. After all, you are his ticket to increasing his fortune, in addition to making yourself a rich man.

HOW TO SET UP YOUR OWN
CORPORATION TO RECEIVE
ALL CAPITAL GAINS

As we mentioned, the risk investor was created by the Internal Revenue Service, and we must take his tax position into consideration in our negotiations. He may be interested in protecting his interest by taking interest-bearing notes from the corporation, or part stock and part notes. Here is where your attorney earns his keep. He can negotiate to form the corporation that will best serve your interest and the investor's interests.

As a safety precaution in case of losses, have your attorney form you as a Sub-Chapter-S Corporation. This enables you to charge all losses to your personal income, which is a benefit if you are in a high income tax bracket.

When your business begins to show considerable profits, you can form a regular corporation, which will help you reap the harvest of capital gains.

But, please remember, tax laws governing corporations are subject to change. Keep in touch with your attorney and your tax accountant. Never trust yourself on tax matters. There is an old saying, "anyone that represents himself as his own attorney has a fool for a client".

THE SECRET, YET LEGAL, WAY TO GET TAX ADVANTAGES YOU WANT

The key here is your tax accountant. It's not enough to learn that you overpaid after your tax returns are filed. You must know, from the day you form your corporation, some of the legal tax shelters to earn extra income for your corporation.

The rule here is to choose the correct fiscal year for your corporation.

For example: If your business starts off by generating large profits, set your fiscal year when you have topped $25,000. This eliminates the surtax for that year. On the other hand, if your corporation is operating at a loss — extend your date a full year to take advantage of any loss carryover.

And, in addition, there is a little known section in the Internal Revenue Code that is often overlooked by small corporations. It allows you to set up a medical plan for corporate members. It allows you to

reimburse a member for all his medical expenses and
to deduct the payments from their personal income
tax.

Make sure your tax accountant has knowledge
of all tax benefits related to your business. A good
C.P.A. can show your investor all the opportunities
for tax savings — and why he should invest in you.

WHERE THE FEDERAL MONEY
IS AND HOW TO
GET YOUR SHARE

Before you decide that your wildest dreams are
beyond your means, just remember that your partner
and closest relative, "Uncle Sam," has many Federal
loan programs that may fit your financial situation.

If one type of loan won't help you, maybe a combination of loans will do the trick. For example,
Junior N. obtained an FHA loan for a new home, then
an SBA loan for a new rain gutter business to be
operated from his garage.

You may meet the requirements for many of the
personal or business loans "Uncle Sam" has to offer.

The rule of thumb guide to see if you qualify is
simple: (1) The loan must be in the interest of the
public; (2) Repayment is assured; (3) And you are
unable to obtain a loan from private or commercial
sources with reasonable terms. The secret here is
"reasonable terms". If the terms are not suitable to
your situation, then a Federal loan could be the
answer to the million dollar business you have been
dreaming about.

In Chapter 2, we gave several tips on "How to
Obtain An SBA Loan." If you are unable to get an
SBA loan, there are other Federal sources that make
business and personal loans. If you live in a town
with less than 50,000 people, the Farmers Home Administration has a loan program for projects that will
benefit the townspeople.

Their offices are usually located in the county seat in your area. Pick up an application, it could be your passport to a business of your own.

And, in addition, if you live in an area which has been designated as economically depressed (and a large percentage of the country has), you may be in line for a loan from the Economic Development Administration. One requirement is you must help increase the employment rate in your community. To get full information, write The Economic Development Administration, Washington, DC.

If you are a veteran, you are in a position to obtain the easiest loan of all, the Veterans Administration Insured Loan. Contact your local V.A. and get all the information available. You may obtain as much as 95% financing on a new home.

As I mentioned, the Farmers Home Administration has programs in cities of less than 50,000 population — but, if you decide to go back to the land or to get out of the rat race, as some people call city life, make a trip to the F.H.A. about purchasing open land or rural property.

However, before you sell out and move to the country, the F.H.A. requires that you were raised on a farm, or have some farm experience before they will consider a loan.

If you own a farm and need a loan to refinance a mortgage, or for improvements, the Farm Credit Administration will be eager to help.

The man down on the farm has many Federal sources from which to obtain capital — take advantage of it. The Agricultural Extension Service in any county seat can supply you with full information.

One of the least known sources of capital used by the small businessman is the Export-Import Bank. Don't let the name scare you off — the bank isn't just for the international "bigs". If you have a business that can or does export its products, this could be your ticket to a fast fortune. The beauty of this type of loan is the credit worthiness, and is based upon the foreign buyer, not you. Get the facts by writing the Export-Import Bank, Washington, DC.

But, that is not all — if you really want to "deal" like a millionaire and become a prospector with a chance to strike it rich in mineral exploration, with your "Uncle Sam" paying half the costs and repayment on a royalty basis, contact the office of Mineral Exploration, Department of the Interior, Washington, DC. They may give you a "grub stake."

The door to the world of finance is open for you and your million dollar ideas — walk on in and you will be welcomed with open arms.

HOW YOU CAN OBTAIN FREE INFORMATION ON MONEY-MAKING DEALS BEFORE THEY REACH THE PUBLIC

Who keeps inside information on almost every money-making proposition? Who keeps records of all patents, copyrights and new products? You guessed it — the United States Government — your government. And rightly it should. But, do you know that you can receive up-to-date information almost on a daily basis — on everything from new bills signed by the president, to what auto or product has been recalled?

This is a publication almost every insider receives — it is called *Consumer News,* and you should be on the mailing list.

It has one section called "S-P-R-E-A-D-I-N-G The Word", all the latest information from money management to warranty updates are published.

Consumer News keeps you on top of all rulings on the Food and Drug Administration, Consumer Products Safety Commission and medical devices.

They even have a section for your comments on various types of new products on the market.

You should write Consumer Information Center, Pueblo, Colorado, 81009 for the subscription rates.

If you wish to receive information before it reaches the general public — I recommend it highly.

But, that's not all — there are other sources of information that our government has to offer you free or at a small printing cost.

FREE MANAGEMENT AIDS

Take your choice of the following publications — they may be obtained at your local Small Business Administration office. Give them a call. They will be eager to send you a copy. And, in addition, you can pick up valuable free business counseling for problems that apply to your new or existing business.

Cash in on this wealth of information. It is a privilege you should exercise as a taxpayer.

#32   How Trade Associations Help Small Business

#41   How the Public Employment Service Helps Small Business

#46   How to Analyze Your Own Business

#49   Know Your Patenting Procedures

#52   Loan Sources in the Federal Government

#53   Small Business Profits from Unpatentable Ideas

#75   Protecting Your Records Against Disaster

#80   Choosing the Legal Structure for Your Firm

#92   Wishing Won't Get Profitable New Products

#111   Steps in Incorporating a Business

#162   Keeping Machines and Operators Productive

SMALL BUSINESSES PAMPHLETS

#1 Handicrafts and Home Businesses

#3 Selling by Mail Order

#9 Marketing Research Procedures

#10 Retailing

#14 The Nursery Business

#15 Recordkeeping Systems — Small Store and Service Trade

#16 Store Location

#17 Restaurants and Catering

#18 Basic Library Reference Sources

#19 Bakery Products

#20 Advertising — Retail Store

#22 Laundry and Dry Cleaning

#23 Training Retail Salespeople

#24 Food Stores

#29 National Mailing-List Houses

#31 Retail Credit and Collections

#32 Selling and Servicing Mechanical Refrigeration and Air Conditioning

#35 Hardware Retailing

#36 Jewelry Retailing

#37 Buying for Retail Stores

#41 Mobile Homes and Parks

#42 Bookstores

#43 Plumbing, Heating and Air Conditioning Job Shop

#44 Job Printing Shop

#45 Men's and Boy's Wear Stores

#46 Woodworking Shops

#48 Furniture Retailing

SMALL BUSINESSMEN'S AIDS

TECHNICAL AIDS

#42 Principles of Plant Layout for Small Plants

#45 Cash Values in Industrial Scrap

#50 Reduce Waste — Increase Profit

#51 Control of Expendable Tools — II

#54 Surface Hardening Practices

#56 Uses of Ceramic Coated Metals in Small Plants

#59 Fire-Fighting Equipment for Small Plants

#60 Noise Reduction in the Small Shop

#62 Cut Corners with Conveyors

#65 Setting Up a Quality Control and Technical Development Laboratory

#67 Keeping Shop Noise from Nearby Residences

#68 Protective Coating for Steel Construction

#70 Is Worker Fatigue Costing You Dollars?

#72 Pointers on Dimensions and Tolerances

#73 Pointers on In-Plant Trucking

#75 Designing for Higher Profits

#76 Tubular Riveting Uses in Small Plants

#77 Are You Using Your Space Effectively?

#78 Controlling Quality in Defense Production

#79 Rented Tools Can Improve Efficiency

#80 Electric Motor Maintenance for Small Plants

#81 In-Plant Storage and Handling of Hazardous Materials

CHAPTER SIX

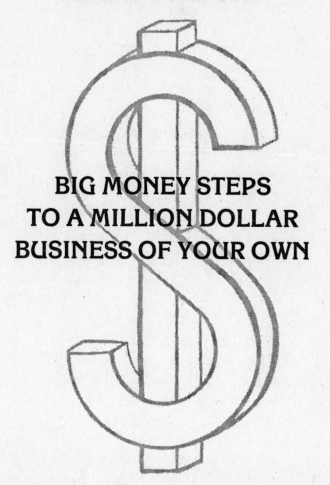

BIG MONEY STEPS
TO A MILLION DOLLAR
BUSINESS OF YOUR OWN

You want to own and manage a million dollar business of your own. That's a great idea, if you know some of the tricks and angles of the trade in advance.

Being your own boss is the dream of many entrepreneurs. However, before you start, ask yourself a few questions. On a separate piece of paper, write the numbers from 1 to 22, then answer each question yes or no. This is your first big money step to a million dollar business of your own.

Be honest with yourself!

1. Are you the kind of person who can get a business started and make it go?
2. Think about why you want to own your own business. Do you want it badly enough to work long hours without knowing how much money you'll end up with?
3. Have you worked in a business like the one you want to start?
4. Have you worked for someone else as a foreman or manager?
5. Have you had any business training in school?
6. Have you saved any money?
7. Do you know how much money you will need to get your business started?
8. Have you counted up how much money of your own you can put into the business?
9. Do you know how much credit you can get from your suppliers — the people you buy from?
10. Do you know where you can borrow the rest of the money you need to start your business?
11. Have you figured out what net income per year you expect to get from the business? Count your salary and your profit on the money you put into the business.
12. Can you live on less than this so that you can use some of it to help your business grow?
13. Have you talked to a banker about your plans?
14. If you need a partner with money or know-how that you don't have, do you know someone who will fit — someone you can get along with?

15. Do you know the good and bad points about going it alone, having a partner, and incorporating your business?

16. Have you talked to a lawyer about it?

17. Do most businesses in your community seem to be doing well?

18. Have you tried to find out whether stores like the one you want to open are doing well in your community and in the rest of the country?

19. Do you know what kind of people will want to buy what you plan to sell?

20. Do people like that live in the area where you plan to open your store?

21. Do they need a store like yours?

22. If not, have you thought about opening a different kind of store and going to another neighborhood?

If most of your answers are "yes", then probably you have what it takes to "deal" like a millionaire in your own busines — *Congratulations!*

HOW TO DEVELOP START-UP TRICKS AND ANGLES TO A FAST FORTUNE

One of the major causes of business failures I have observed in my years in the financial world was the wasting of money on unnecessary items during the start-up process. If you ask any man who has failed in business, he will tell you "my expenses ate up my profits".

This brings us to a most useful start-up trick in your business — I will call it an "expense statement."

You should have, on your desk at the end of each week, an expense statement showing where every dime was spent. They should be summarized at the end of the month and compared with the previous month's expenses.

One of the early dangers in almost every new business is what is called a "catch all." This is where various and sundry expenses are lumped together as general expense. It hides a lot of waste in your business — eliminate it.

Every entrepreneur should divide his expenses into minute categories. This way, you can detect the leaks in your outgoing cash and put a stop to them.

Every man who develops "start up tricks and angles" to a fast fortune in his own business must have a statement of both receipts and expenses. This puts you in the pilot's seat. A pilot doesn't seem to do much until an emergency. Then he shows his skill and training. You will be able to do the same. You can see the weak spots and make repairs before disaster strikes.

If you keep close tabs on your income with an income sheet and an expense statement, you won't have to worry about a plus or minus. You can see at a glance where the profit is coming from and where expenses are being leaked.

Always remember, the only real success that comes to you as a businessman is the net profits at the end of the year.

If you are really interested in "start up angles" — you will take your items of expense separately — go over the payroll costs, cost of utilities and cost of merchandise. However, don't assume you are paying too much for everything. Use good "horse sense" and see whether you are getting value received for your money.

Take salaries — is the employee producing enough to warrant his salary, plus a profit for the company? Can one employee do the work of two? You should get full production from each employee. Remember, the best paid employees are often the least expensive, because you can afford to pay the productive workers more if they can make or save you money.

The matter of expenses is most important to the newcomer in this "Be Your Own Boss" free enterprise system.

In addition to keeping a check on expenses, you must make purchases of materials and goods to stock your shelves. Then, you must use "start up angles and tricks" as a buyer.

To become a good buyer, you can gain much information by watching the salesman's methods.

Some businessmen think that being belligerent, rude, or telling plain lies make a salesman "cow down" so that the businessman can get a better deal. This is far from the truth. For example, I had the pleasure to make a business loan to Pat S., follow his progress in his new business, and watch him use angles with salesmen who called at his place of business.

First, Pat was a gentleman. He kept his promises and he knew his business thoroughly. He was always truthful with a salesman. He let them know that for him to stay in business, he had to get as much value for his dollar as possible. And, if they were to continue doing business together, it meant fairness to both.

One angle he used in making purchases from a salesman was that he always let the salesman know that the better he treated him in price and quality, the more the savings could be passed on to Pat's customers. This would allow them to continue to do business in the future. In addition to that, he let the salesman know he could get the best of him once or twice, but no more than that.

You can be a successful businessman if you gain a good knowledge of the products you intend to purchase for your business. One of the most valuable things a businessman should know is where the factory is located that makes the goods, and he should get the factory cost where possible. Another start-up trick is to learn from your competitors which salesmen or companies have the best reputation for service or guarantees on products you buy.

Pat once told me that when you find a supplier who is *oversold* (so that you must place back-orders) he has a tendency to become independent. But, a supplier who needs the business will give you the red carpet treatment.

Make a few phone calls if you are not satisfied with present suppliers or factory. It will help you on your way to building your million dollar business.

HOW TO BE BOSS — WITHOUT A FOOL FOR AN EMPLOYER — AND STILL MAKE A PROFIT

The success of your business depends largely upon the example set by you — THE BOSS.

If you are negligent in your responsibilities, use sharp-tongued business practices, and your business then goes bankrupt, it was most likely brought on by employees who followed the boss's example.

If he sets a good example his business will prosper.

There isn't one chance in a thousand of your business becoming a success unless you learn how to be the boss — without a fool for an employer.

To set the example:

1. *The boss must know the job he hires an employee to do, or have trained personnel to teach the new employee.*

2. *The boss must point out employee errors kindly — showing a better way to do the job when possible.*

3. The boss should show interest in his employee's welfare, his family, and his desires. The employee will repay a hundredfold.
4. The boss should want to remain aloof. He should be just far enough above to be Captain.
5. The boss should be approachable, and listen to employee's grievances.
6. The boss should talk with employees — not down to them.

Remember, if your business is to make a profit, the boss must learn he can't run a million dollar business by himself. The only business he could run by himself would probably be an organ grinder's job — then he still would need a monkey to collect the money.

To make a profit you need hardworking and loyal employees.

If you — the boss — set the example of a dependable, generous and kindly person — not a fool — your business will make a profit.

But that's not all. You can know in advance if you have the potential to be the boss. Start by taking the following quiz, prepared by the SBA. See if you have the personal characteristics to be boss of your own business.

Take a separate sheet of note paper, and then check the answers that come closest to what you feel.

Again, be honest with yourself.

Are You a Self-Starter?
A. I do things on my own. Nobody has to tell me to get going.
B. If someone gets me started, I keep going all right.
C. Easy does it, man. I don't put myself out until I have to.

How Do You Feel About Other People?

A. I like people. I can get along with just about anybody.

B. I have plenty of friends — I don't need anyone else.

C. Most people bug me.

Can You Lead Others?

A. I can get most people to go along when I start something.

B. I can give the orders if someone tells me what we should do.

C. I let someone else get things moving. Then I go along if I feel like it.

Can You Take Responsibility?

A. I like to take charge of things and see them through.

B. I'll take over if I have to, but I'd rather let someone else be responsible.

C. There's always some eager beaver around wanting to show how smart he is. I say let him.

How Good an Organizer Are You?

A. I like to have a plan before I start. I'm usually the one to get things lined up when the gang wants to do something.

B. I do all right unless things get too goofed up. Then I cop out.

C. You get all set and then something comes along and blows the whole bag. So, I just take things as they come.

How Good a Worker Are You?

A. I can keep going as long as I need to. I don't mind working hard for something I want.

    B. *I'll work hard for a while, but when I've had enough, that's it, man!*

    C. *I can't see that hard work gets you anywhere.*

Can You Make Decisions?

    A. *I can make up my mind in a hurry if I have to. It usually turns out O.K., too.*

    B. *I can if I have plenty of time. If I have to make up my mind fast, I think later I should have decided the other way.*

    C. *I don't like to be the one who has to decide things. I'd probably blow it.*

Can People Trust What You Say?

    A. *You bet they can. I don't say things I don't mean.*

    B. *I try to be on the level most of the time, but sometimes I just say what's easiest.*

    C. *What's the sweat if the other fellow doesn't know the difference?*

Can You Stick with It?

    A. *If I make up my mind to do something, I don't let anything stop me.*

    B. *I usually finish what I start — if it doesn't get fouled up.*

    C. *If it doesn't go right away, I turn off. Why beat your brains out?*

How Good Is Your Health?

    A. *Man, I never run down!*

    B. *I have enough energy for most things I want to do.*

    C. *I run out of juice sooner than most of my friends do.*

Now count the checks you made.

How many checks are there beside the first answer to each question?

How many checks are there beside the second answer to each question?

How many checks are there beside the third answer to each question?

If most of your checks are beside the "A" answer, you probably have what it takes to run a business, and be your own boss.

Now, lets take another big money step to a million dollar business of our own.

A FOOLPROOF CHECKLIST FOR GOING INTO BUSINESS THAT WILL SAVE YOU $$$ IN START UP CASH

You passed the "Be Your Own Boss" quiz with flying colors. Again, congratulations are in order. Where do you go from here? Everyone who wishes to build a million dollar business is faced with the question sooner or later. The natural thing is to seek ways to obtain the start up cash. However, before you rush to our bank or venture capital source, take one more trial quiz. Take the same sheet of note paper, and answer the following questions "yes" or "no."

Your Building

1. *Have you found a good building for your store?*
2. *Will you have enough room when your business gets bigger?*
3. *Can you fix the building the way you want it without spending too much money?*
4. *Can people get to it easily from parking spaces, bus stops or their homes?*

5. Have you had a lawyer check the lease and zoning laws?

Equipment and Supplies

1. Do you know just what equipment and supplies you need and how much they will cost?

Your Merchandise

1. Have you decided what things you will sell?
2. Do you know how much or how many of each you will buy to open your store with?
3. Have you found suppliers who will sell you what you need at a good price?
4. Have you compared the prices and credit terms of different suppliers?

Your Records

1. Have you planned a system of records that will keep track of income and expenses, what you owe other people, and what other people owe you?
2. Have you worked out a way to keep track of your inventory so that you will always have enough on hand for your customers, but not more than you can sell?
3. Have you figured out how to keep your payroll records and take care of tax reports and payments?
4. Do you know what financial statements you should prepare?
5. Do you know how to use these financial statements?
6. Do you know an accountant who will help you with your records and financial statements?

Your Store and the Law

1. Do you know what licenses and permits you need?
2. Do you know what business laws you have to obey?
3. Do you know a lawyer you can go to for advice and for help with legal papers?

Protecting Your Store

1. Have you made plans for protecting your store against thefts of all kinds — shoplifting, robbery, burglary, employee stealing?
2. Have you talked with an insurance agent about what kinds of insurance you need?

Buying a Business Someone Else Has Started

1. Have you made a list of what you like and don't like about buying a business someone else has started?
2. Are you sure you know the real reason why the owner wants to sell his business?
3. Have you compared the cost of buying the business with the cost of starting a new business?
4. Is the stock up to date and in good condition?
5. Is the building in good condition?
6. Will the owner of the building transfer the lease to you?
7. Have you talked with other businessmen in the area to see what they think of the business?
8. Have you talked with the company's suppliers?
9. Have you talked with a lawyer about it?

Advertising

1. Have you decided how you will advertise

(Newspapers — posters — handbills — radio — by mail)?

2. Do you know where to get help with your ads?
3. Have you watched what other stores do to get people to buy?

The Prices You Charge

1. Do you know how to figure what you should charge for each item you sell?
2. Do you know what other stores like yours charge?

Buying

1. Do you have a plan for finding out what your customers want?
2. Will your plan for keeping track of your inventory tell you when it is time to order more and how much to order?
3. Do you plan to buy most of your stock from a few suppliers, rather than a little from many, so that those you buy from will want to help you succeed?

Selling

1. Have you decided whether you will have sales clerks or self service?
2. Do you know how to get customers to buy?
3. Have you thought about why you like to buy from some salesmen, while others turn you off?

Your Employees

1. If you need to hire someone to help you, do you know where to look?
2. Do you know what kind of person you need?
3. Do you know how much to pay?

4. *Do you have a plan for training your employees?*

Credit for Your Customers

1. *Have you decided whether to let your customers buy on credit?*
2. *Do you know the good and bad points about joining a credit card plan?*
3. *Can you tell a deadbeat from a good credit customer?*

If you have answered all these questions carefully, you've done some hard work and serious thinking. That's good.

Now we are ready to visit your money source. Prepare a personal financial statement. (Forms may be obtained at your bank.) Then make a copy of the following "estimated monthly expenses" checklist. Take both to your banker — This will show you have done your homework.

You have taken another big money step to a business of your own.

$$ How John F. Uses His Banker to Get Rich on Borrowed Money

Every new business will run into tough sledding financially at some time, and it will have to borrow money to tide it over some of the rough spots. Try to anticipate your borrowing needs in advance — just as John F. in Bakersfield, California, who borrowed money when he didn't need it. John has a close relationship with the loan manager of a bank — He will often borrow money and repay in 30 days to build a good credit standing. Each time he increases the amount he wishes to borrow until he has a good credit limit established. Then, when a rainy day comes, he obtains the necessary capital without any delay.

And, in addition, John F. has developed a relationship with his bank so that he can overdraw his bank account for a few days without any charge. In other words, he can write checks that won't bounce. However, John calls the bank in advance and discusses his problem with the loan manager.

As we mentioned, the closer the relationship you have with your bank, the better chance you have to get special favors when needed.

Always be courteous to all bank employees and learn their names. You will be surprised how much tellers will help you when they are addressed politely and by name.

But that isn't all. Your banker handles money problems, just as a lawyer handles legal problems. When you have a money problem, you see your banker. He may have a solution you never heard of.

Your banker is an expert in money matters — take advantage of it. You will improve not only your relationship, but your borrowing power as well.

FULL RANGE OF BANK SERVICES THAT PUTS CASH IN YOUR POCKET — AND IN YOUR BANK ACCOUNT

Often, when you walk into a bank to open a business account, you are directed to the new account department and your business account is handled by a clerk. You never get to talk to a VP who can outline the requirements needed for your business. Here is a tip. Always phone the loan manager of the bank before you go in. This gives you an opportunity to find out the special services the bank has to offer its customers.

For example, if you sell hard goods or high-ticket items, you will need contract dealer financing. If the bank doesn't provide this service, you will want to shop around. Also, if the bank has a department for installment contract sales, he can give you quicker

ESTIMATED MONTHLY EXPENSES

Item	Your estimate of monthly expenses based on sales of $_____ per year	Your estimate of how much cash you need to start your business. (see column 3)	What to put in column 2 (these figures are typical for one kind of business. You will have to decide how many months to allow for in your business
	Column 1	Column 2	Column 3
Salary of owner-manager	$	$	2 times column 1
All other salaries and wages			3 times column 1
Rent			3 times column 1
Advertising			3 times column 1
Delivery expense			3 times column 1

Supplies		3 times column 1
Telephone		3 times column 1
Other utilities		3 times column 1
Insurance		Payment required by insurance company
Taxes		4 times column 1
Interest		3 times column 1
Maintenance		3 times column 1
Legal fees		3 times column 1
Miscellaneous		3 times column 1
TOTALS	$	$

121

ESTIMATED MONTHLY EXPENSES

	Column 2	Column 3
Enter total Column 2 from previous page	$	
STARTING COSTS YOU ONLY HAVE TO PAY ONCE		
Fixtures and equipment	$	Estimate what you'll need
Decorating and remodeling		Talk it over with a contractor
Installation of fixtures and equipment		Talk to suppliers from whom you'll buy these
Starting inventory		Suppliers will probably help you estimate this
Deposits with public utilities		Find out from utilities companies
Legal and other professional fees		Lawyer, accountant, etc.

Licenses and permits		Find out from city offices what you have to have
Advertising and promotion for opening		Estimate what you'll use
Accounts receivable		What you need to buy more stock until credit customers pay
Cash		For unexpected expenses or losses, special purchases, etc.
Other		Make separate list & enter total
TOTAL ESTIMATED CASH YOU NEED TO START	$	Add up all numbers in Column 2

approval, which in turn enables you to service your customers faster. It also puts cash in your pocket.

The best rule to follow in locating a bank that can give you special service to meet your business needs is to find out which bank your competitor uses.

You will soon discover in shopping around for banks that many don't want small business accounts, but prefer the large corporation. However, they aren't going to come out and tell you this. If they aren't eager for your business, you should assume they prefer larger accounts. Here are a few questions to ask your bank VP:

1. *Does the bank place a limit on small business loans — if so, how much?*
2. *What are the qualifications for a bank line of credit?*
3. *Will you have to keep a certain checking account balance to obtain a loan?*
4. *What is their policy on cashing large checks — (this is important, because if they hold a check several days for collection before crediting your account, several of your checks could bounce.)*

You may not get straight answers to your questions, but you will get enough information to know if you want to establish your business account with them.

And, in addition, if you sell on credit — take advantage of the credit card services offered. There are several cards available; try to find a bank who handles the majority. It will save time as you would otherwise be making several report deposits to various banks. Please remember, a credit card sale is like a cash sale, minus a small fee.

As I mentioned, you want to use the full range of bank services to put cash in your pockets — and in your bank accounts.

HOW TO OBTAIN INSTANT NEW CREDIT AND USE LIKE CASH IN YOUR BANK

The businessman who says "I want no credit — I buy and sell for cash," is making a mistake. No single factor is more important than credit in building your business.

Establish a credit rating whether you need it or not — it is good advertising.

Establishing credit is fairly easy to do — the start-up trick is to keep it. Pay promptly, because credit is like cash in your bank. You are using other people's money to increase your business. Also, arranging credit with your suppliers is often difficult if you are unable to furnish a bank reference.

If your suppliers are small business men — present them with a financial statement and use the start-up angle that Greg P. used to obtain instant credit from a clothing wholesaler. When he presented his financial statement to the credit manager, he informed him, "I always pay my bills on receipt of the statement," and "If for any reason, you wish to discuss my account, call me personally at home. My unlisted phone number is 123-4567. Please put it in your files for future reference..." This simple trick has helped Greg open accounts with wholesalers when other businessmen have been rejected.

Some of the larger suppliers hesitate to open a line of credit to a new business. Try this. Have them ship to you C.O.D. (make arrangements beforehand for a business loan at your bank to cover purchases). After a few shipments, they will set up a line of credit for your business.

As I mentioned, credit is fairly easy to obtain, but the trick is to keep it. Pay promptly. This not only builds your good rating, but you can take advantage of all discounts. This puts cash in your pocket.

Suppose you become slow in paying your bills. There are a few angles to help keep your good credit. When you get a curt letter from your creditor demanding the balance of your account, phone him if possible, and tell him what date he can expect a payment. Don't give the exact amount you plan to pay, unless you can keep your promise — but give him a specific date — and make sure your check is there on time.

Please remember this, as long as your creditor gets something on the account by the time promised — it helps keep him in a good mood. It is the businessman who breaks his promise who receives a hard time from his creditors.

There is a saying among bankers and creditors — "K.I.T." *Keep In Touch* with your debtors. Use this in reverse — K.I.T. with your creditors. Let them know that you are a good moral risk. Suppliers and creditors have hearts. Remember, without credit customers they would be out of business. They want you as a customer.

Be honest and frank. Tell your creditor that you will soon be on your feet and will make larger purchases. He will have an interest in your business.

As I mentioned, the small bank or creditor is the best place for a new businessman to obtain credit. Usually, the big banks or suppliers are indifferent, and often your account is handled by a clerk who remembers you only as an account number.

Credit is like cash in the bank, its use or abuse determines your business success or failure.

If your credit rating is bad, there are steps to get it reestablished. First, go to your local credit bureau where you can see your credit file. Find out which stores are reporting slow credit. Second, go to the store manager and find out how you can build up your record again with them. You might tell them your financial position is better now, and you wish to reestablish your credit with the store. If you want a new start, go to a bank that has Visa or MasterCharge and open a checking account. Try to keep over a $100.00 in your account at all times. When you can, obtain one of their credit cards. Also, try to get a credit card from a gas company. Use them as references. Soon your credit will be reestablished. Remember this, pay on time and don't overextend, or you will be right back with a negative credit rating.

Remember these things as you take big money steps to a million dollar business of your own. Keep In Touch (K.I.T.), with your creditors. Credit is based on trust more than on a bank account.

Make partial payments when you can't pay in full. Be honest. When you are financially strong, stick with those who stuck with you. If you practice these virtues, suppliers, wholesalers, bankers and creditors will be knocking at the door of your million dollar business.

LITTLE-KNOWN ANGLES TO GET FREE ADVERTISING FOR YOUR NEW BUSINESS

If you have a good thing, you must tell about it. Telling makes selling. Telling is simply advertising, and advertising is what makes your business grow.

When we speak of advertising, we refer to everything that makes an impression on your prospective customer. This can be paid advertising, or your reputation as an honest businessman.

You must advertise to be successful in your business.

The best free advertising for a new business is what is known as a "press release." For example, when Don W. opened his pharmacy in a small town, he took a picture of his new building before the grand opening, with his manager standing beneath his sign.

He had the local photo shop blow his picture up to an 8X10 black and white glossy print.

Then, he prepared a short story about his background, telling where he graduated as a pharmaceutical student and all the civic clubs he belonged to. He also included the grand opening date of his pharmacy.

This was typed and double spaced with the heading "For Release on (month—day)." It was then delivered to his local newspaper, along with the picture — and it was in print at no cost to Don.

Take your local newspaper and read closely. You will find that most of the news came about through press releases. You will also get some good ideas for your own grand opening.

INSIDE TRICKS YOU SHOULD KNOW AS BOSS THAT WILL MAKE YOU THINK LIKE A MILLIONAIRE

The man whose memory allows him to play six games of checkers at the same time is good for nothing else. There are bookkeepers who can name every customer's previous bank balance, but they can never "deal" like a millionaire. The dollar knows nothing about mental gymnastics.

That is why a good businessman doesn't rely on his memory — but relies on his ability to find out about things and get results.

If you remember only slow-paying customers, how can you remember the good customers who pay promptly each month? If you could pick a rich man's pocket — you would find it filled with little written notes. Make a habit of writing yourself notes, fold them up, and put them in your pocket. Let the notes do the memory work, while your mind is thinking of how to turn another deal like a millionaire.

Richard E., who travels for an insurance company, has a unique way to remember important things to do. While he is traveling, he writes himself postcards and mails them each day. When he arrives home the following week, the postcards have done all the heavy mental work.

Don't trust your memory. If you think of something important, jot it down on a pad. Or, as a friend of mine does, use a small pocket recorder, which you can play back at the end of each business day.

Memory is a bad employee. Have employees write down figures. Never make a deal where dollars are involved unless the amount is written down. You or your customer may have heard the wrong dollar amounts.

As you think like a millionaire, never trust a mental memo. When you have a written memo, you have the facts. A memo pad seldom forgets, and it is available at your command.

Pencils and paper are too inexpensive for us to take a chance on forgetting a million dollar deal.

CHAPTER SEVEN

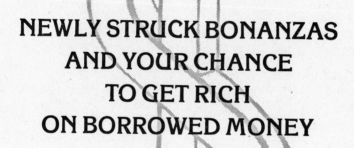

NEWLY STRUCK BONANZAS
AND YOUR CHANCE
TO GET RICH
ON BORROWED MONEY

At this very moment, there are hundreds of ways for ordinary people like you and me to finance our first venture in real estate. I will show you how to make borrowed money work for you as you begin to build a real estate empire.

First, as a beginner, you should buy income-producing properties and start a growing rental income. This newly struck bonanza has made many a millionaire. There is nothing hard about investing in income property. You can do it without a cent of your own.

HOW TO GET RICH ON BORROWED MONEY WITH INCOME PRODUCING PROPERTY

Once you obtain a piece of property with an income which exceeds the expenses, you can make a fortune using *leverage* to its fullest.

Leverage is the money-getting power secret of many bankers. This is the way to make your invested capital increase its working power.

Leverage is credit — Leverage is credit. I repeat this because it is a powerful force for making money fast.

For example, if you buy a tract of land for $5,000 and later sell it for $10,000, you make 100% profit. *Now watch leverage* work. You buy the same tract for $500 down and $500 a year in payments. In one year, you sell the land for the same price of $10,000. You invested $1,000 (cost plus payments), and after paying the $4,000 balance, you have the same profit of $5,000, but that is 500% profit on your investment.

For example, investing in apartments has made Ike R., a former musician, a wealthy man. He started with a single family residence, traded his equity for a duplex, then began the trade-up technique by using the money-getting power of leverage. Ike took possession of his duplex, fixed it up, increased the rental income, and then used the equity as leverage to trade up to a four-plex. He began to repeat the process. Picking up larger units on each trade until he owned a 40-unit apartment complex.

You can use the same money-making process for getting rich with income-producing property. However, you may want to test and work your own plan for success and prosperity before you actually lay out any money.

For example, try this test. If you are a home

owner, find out from your mortgage holder the amount of equity you have in your home. Then check out the realty sales section of your local paper. Find a duplex for sale and contact the owner or his agent. Explain the amount of equity you have in your home and discuss what kind of deal he will make on the duplex. You will be surprised at how easy it is to trade for income-producing property. Often, the realtor will do all the leg and paper work. Check out several duplexes. You will gain confidence and experience.

After all, you don't have anything to lose, because you haven't signed any contracts. Then again, you may receive an offer you can't refuse, as you are on your road to "dealing" like a millionaire.

The quick way to make money in apartments (without any money) is to hunt for high-priced properties that are for sale. Then, go to a lender and ask him to appraise the property on the basis of a mortgage with longer terms than the one that exists on the property, say 10 years longer. They come up with a figure that is the same as the asking price, but because the mortgage is 10 years longer, payments are less. If it brings in $24,000 net on a $2 million property, what do you have? Well, you have $24,000 in income, a free apartment and an equity in a $2 million project.

If you really want to "deal" like a millionaire, you could print up some fancy business cards, contact the seller and hand him your card. Tell him you will buy on a "no cash" deal and let him make the financing arrangements and handle the transaction. You may get laughed at several times, but all it takes is nerve. Keep asking until someone says "yes". You will be surprised at how many deals you can pick up this way.

I must also tell you that there are very few people trying to buy multi-million dollar properties, which eliminates competition at the top. If you don't mind the rebuffs, you can strike a bonanza and get rich on borrowed money.

THE MAGIC ART OF FINDING
A GIANT FORTUNE IN LAND

Ninety percent of all millionaires become so through owning real estate. This is more than in all industrial investments combined. The wise man of today invests his money in real estate.

A tract of land can't run away; a thief can't steal it and you can't burn it up or down — it is the most permanent investment you can make, and is the greatest source of all wealth. The growing scarcity of usable land makes it an investor's bonanza because there isn't any more being made.

What creates the value of land? Values are created by people using the land. The more people who use it, the more valuable it becomes. The tract of land that offers the investor the best opportunity for capital appreciation is raw land.

Raw land can be subdivided into residential, commercial or industrial lots. In this way, it can be put to the fullest use. Population growth always forces land values up.

The magic of finding a giant fortune in land is to just follow the path of growth. The line of growth will always be greater along highways and will extend toward the next population center, the next town or city. If you wish to speculate in land, get in on the line of growth.

Here are some pointers:

1. *Older sections always tend to get worse.*

2. *High class residential areas tend to grow along easy access roads.*

3. *As you look for land, remember that you are speculating in land and the structures are of*

no value to you. You are buying for develop-
ment and not for personal use.

4. *One cardinal rule: Never buy land you have*
never walked on. It could be under water, a
swamp, or on top of a mountain without a
road. Investigate before you invest.

But that's not all. Take a tip from a banker. How many small town bankers do you know who don't own a good bottom land farm? No man ever bought good farm or grass land and lost money in the long run. It's true that at different times of the year, prices may go up or down, but if you let a farm produce a bumper crop or you get a good grass lease, you can just watch the price of your land go up.

The beauty of good farm land is that you can always go to the bank and borrow up to 90% of its value. If you want to strike a new bonanza, buy land that produces some kind of crop, even if it's only a small tract to begin.

There is a difference in land that produces something and a vacant city lot. The vacant lot doesn't bring in anything, and you are hoping it will increase in value.

Real estate booms come in cycles, and there is property in every town that is worth more today than it was ten years ago.

I agree that there are prime sections of cities where property value will continue to rise slowly. But please remember that the same amount of money invested at 10% will give you a greater return for your dollar.

I have one bank customer, Alfred R., who buys only farm or grass land that he can lease. It will always pay him an income, and good land always increases in value.

When you buy land that produces something, you are exchanging your cash for the basis of all wealth. The crops that are produced are exchanged for money, and you are really growing money out of the ground.

$$ How a Business Loan (File #112) Brought 4,000 People from 5 States to put Money in James R's Pocket

I am going to share some newly struck bonanzas with you from my private files, and ideas that came from entrepreneurs who came to the bank seeking business loans. I have changed the names of the customers, because all business loans are confidential. In addition, I have selected business loan requests that represent highly successful ideas, along with some that have no merit at all. I have done this to give you an opportunity to see that people of all backgrounds are making efforts to get rich on borrowed money.

If you find an idea you can use, develop it and present it to your local bank. It could be a bonanza for you.

Confidential Business Loan (File #112). James R. had no money, but had a great idea. To help carry out his money-making plan, the bank advanced enough money for James to purchase a 7,000 square foot circus tent. The purpose was to set up what he called a "Flea Circus." He leased a two-acre plot of ground and erected the huge tent. Incidentally, large crowds came just to watch the big top erected.

James had 4 X 8 foot tables built and placed under the tent, which he rented by the day. Also, he had portable buildings that were rented by the month.

He had a concession stand that served hot dogs and cold drinks, and there was a tape system that played circus music.

He advertised as the "World's Largest Big Top Flea Circus", and on opening day he had 4,000 people from five states pass through his flea market. Traffic was backed up for a mile, waiting for a parking space.

James had a local high school boy dressed up as a clown, handing out balloons and favors to the children. It was an instant success.

If you really like excitement and a chance to strike it rich on borrowed money, you might consider a "Big Top Flea Circus." It could be a fortune that has been waiting for you.

$$ How Bennie C. Uses Inside Bank Secret to Collect 50% of Abandoned Estates

Confidential Business Loan (File #37). Bennie C., an employee of a large metropolitan bank, uses a little-known secret to locate missing heirs.

In most cases, a bank, cannot under law, open the safety deposit box of a person who has died until the IRS has had a chance to inventory its contents.

Armed with this knowledge and the fact that the estate of an individual reverts to the state if an heir doesn't claim it after a certain period of time, Bennie starts searching for the heir.

Once the heir is located, he agrees to split the estate fifty-fifty.

Here is how you can do the same thing.

Go to the state Capital and find out where you can look over *Unclaimed Estates* and pick out one or two for starters. When locating an heir, *we work backwards.* Begin with the death certificate; get his last address; check out his friends; find out if he belonged to any lodges, etc. Make up a listing sheet on the deceased. Keep working back, and soon you will locate a marriage license or a birth certificate, and eventually, you will find an heir.

Just a little tip! *Don't tell the heir* where you have located the estate until you have a written contract signed.

This is a business you can get into with only a telephone and a little savvy. If you are good at tracing missing persons, why not do it for big money, tracing *missing heirs*. Incidentally, Bennie obtained a loan for a round trip ticket to Puerto Rico to sign a contract with an heir for $90,000.

$$ How Mary W. Earns $100 a Week for Two Hours Work a Day

Confidential Business Loan (File #37). Mary Williams, a former bank teller, was the type of girl who wanted to be her own boss. She came to the bank and borrowed $80 to purchase a sales kit to sell cosmetics via the home party plan. After learning the ropes of party plan selling, she set up shop for herself.

She came to my office two weeks after leaving her bank job to tell me she was only working two hours a day and was netting $100 a week.

Mary's husband was quitting his sales job to join her full time. They expect their income in six months to hit $35,000.

Here is how she explained it to me.

Mary had her own brand name cosmetic line, and had 22 distributors working for her.

She told me you could get your own brand name cosmetics from Solo Labs, Inc., Chicago, IL 60624 — Custom Cosmetics, 4848 Farrogut, Brooklyn, NY 11203.

If you like party plan selling, why not sell your own product and strike your own bonanza. You could make all the money you need.

$$ How David M. Receives an Automatic Income for Life — Without Working

Confidential Business Loan (File #49). In the course of a day in the lending business, you see many unusual ways that entrepreneurs make money. David M. was no exception. The day he requested a loan to buy shares in a fish farm, I was skeptical.

He presented a publication entitled "The Livestock That Swims", which he had obtained from the University of Texas at Austin. After close examination, I could see the possibilities.

David and a few friends had formed a co-op to raise catfish, along the same principle as investors in Texas and Colorado, who own cattle feed lots.

Once the fish farm was in operation, David received his share of each harvest — and he never catches a fish. If you are interested, write the University of Texas for a copy of the publication "The Livestock That Swims".

Remember, fish farming has struggled along for years as a backyard enterprise, but now it is beginning to show promise as a big business in the U.S.

Most of the trout available at your supermarket didn't come from sparkling streams, they were raised on large trout farms in the south and west. It is estimated that 95% of the catfish sold in the U.S. come from small ponds on family acreages or elaborate fish farms similar to the one David invested in which are worth hundreds of thousands of dollars.

It is possible that the Small Business Administration could help finance your fish farm.

If you like the outdoors and like to fish, you may parlay a few thousand dollars into a fortune.

$$ Other Confidential Business Loans — Making Money for Entrepreneurs

Confidential Business Loan (File #134). Here is an unusual loan request. Patricia M., a former hair stylist, needed $200 to purchase a male poodle dog. Here is a new twist on raising and selling poodles.

Patricia says poodles are temperamental, like children. So, she lets her prospective customers adopt a poodle.

She interviews a customer, explaining that she has to match the poodle to the new owner. She asks several questions, how they plan to keep the dog happy, and so on, then she shows them the poodle best suited to their disposition.

Patricia then lets them adopt the poodle for a price. She has printed adoption certificates and offers a month's free consultation if any problems arise. This makes the owner and the poodle something special. It could be a way to strike a bonanza in the poodle business.

Confidential Business Loan (File #135). A few weeks ago, a representative of a large department store in a shopping center, visited Robert W., a real estate salesman, and made this proposition.

He offered to rent floor space on a percentage basis if he would put in a business that could increase the store's volume.

Robert surveyed the store and found that many departments were leased by independent business people, and for all the store benefits, they only paid a percentage of gross sales.

While in the store, he noticed a large fabric department and not a sewing machine anywhere around. The store gave him a small area of floor space near the fabric department.

He then made arrangements for a business loan (File #135) to purchase several name brand sewing machines, and is doing a land office business.

This is an easy way to get into business on borrowed money and in another person's store. Check out some large department stores. They may be looking for someone to give floor space to, in order to increase their profits. You can get into this highly profitable, wide open field with practically no money of your own.

Confidential Business Loan (File #161). Remember the old days, when the neighbors would all pitch in and raise a barn, or harvest a crop for a neighbor?

Jessie M., of Ft. Worth, Texas, has the same principle working for him, painting houses.

No, he doesn't paint the house. Jessie sells the paint. He borrows the money to purchase the paint wholesale at a local hardware store. Here is how he works:

He runs a small ad in the newspaper "*Your House Painted — All You Buy Is The Paint — Please call this phone number...*"

He is flooded with calls, and he tells the caller that he is forming a small group (4 or 5 people) to paint each other's houses. He explains how 4 or 5 people can paint a house in one day, and all he is out is the cost of the paint. If the caller doesn't want to paint, Jessie finds a substitute for so much an hour.

They paint two or three houses a week, with Jessie as supervisor, and he sells a truckload of paint.

You may think of other ways to use this principle to strike a bonanza.

Confidential Business Loan (File #231). This is one of the most unusual business loans we made to a professional man.

Bob F., an attorney on our Board of Directors, is a "carney" at heart. Every summer, he would put his law books up and travel with a carnival. Here is how Bob does it:

He never gets out of a 200-mile range from home. He comes home almost every night, and makes good money with a kiddie airplane ride he bought, and for which he borrowed every penny. He tells me that many of the small carnivals that operate in shopping centers are eager to rent you space.

How do you find out what type of attraction to start with? He gave me what he calls, *The Bible of the Carney's.* It is a book that has hundreds of attractions, from a ferris wheel to a fun house. You can get one if you send a request to A & B Enterprises,

Box 875, Peoria, Illinois 61601. Who knows, you might wind up with your own carnival.

Confidential Business Loan (File #76). Wilma W. is a person who always wanted to do her own thing, and now at the age of 60, she is making more money than she ever made in her life. The rewards she has received from borrowed money have uplifted her to a whole new life.

She obtained a business loan to purchase a beautiful 19th century remanufactured popcorn wagon. That's right, a popcorn wagon. Recently, we attended an outside art festival in Oklahoma City, and there was Wilma, making more money than any of the art dealers. She was doing a landslide business selling popcorn at 50¢ a bag.

She tells me it is easy for her to take in $25,000 a year.

Something to think about — large shopping malls or department stores might rent you space.

If you would like information on the wagon, write C. Cretorr and Company, 620 West Cermack Road, Chicago, Illinois 60616.

Confidential Business Loan (File #216). If you are a camera bug, take a tip from Charles F., who came up with this unique idea for making money.

After he borrowed $150 to purchase a camera, he began to take pictures of points of interest in his home town. He then selected the best twelve pictures for a home town calendar.

Charles contacted a local printer, which used offset printing to print calendar sheets for him — They were attached to the bottom of the pictures he had taken.

The result was a beautiful calendar for the home folks.

Here is where Charles made his money. He sold AD SPACE to the local businessmen who gave the calendar to their customers. Everyone in town wanted copies — not only for themselves, but to send to former residents.

Confidential Business Loan (File #86). Direct selling is a field you can get in with little or no money. Age is no barrier. You can be your own boss and set your own hours. You can earn a commission or buy wholesale and sell retail. There are several ways to sell a customer: (1) appointments; (2) door to door; (3) route; (4) party plan; (5) referral.

You can sell anything from books to brushes. Sales aids and personal help are often available from the manufacturers. Many retired persons, teenagers, businessmen, housewives, students, in fact, approximately 3,500,000 people earn extra pocket money in direct sales.

There are many companies such as Avon, Tupperware, Encyclopedia Britannica, Fuller Brush, Beeline Fashions, and many others that are anxious to help anyone interested in selling their products.

Pearson J., a bank customer of ours, borrowed enough money to purchase a franchise on a regular burglar alarm system. Now, with three salesmen, he averages $1,000 a week.

If you would like the excitement of direct selling, write Direct Selling Association, 1730 M Street, NW, Washington, D. C., 20036, for their list of DSA members. Be sure to enclose a self-addressed stamped envelope. This could set you up with enough money and security to last the rest of your life.

Confidential Business Loan (File #163). A most unusual real estate loan was made to Leham M., who purchased a five-acre tract in eastern Oklahoma, with an unmarked grave which was rumored to be the burial ground of an Indian tribe.

Leham began to sell an undivided "one inch" of real estate in an authentic Indian burial ground. He had legal deeds to give each purchaser. The idea was "for the man who had everything".

Each plot (one inch) was sold for $10. How many plots were sold? We don't know, but stop and think how many square inches there in a five acre tract of land!!

Could there be an unusual historical piece of ground in your area? Why not sell it in undivided inches. This is one newly struck bonanza, with a little borrowed money, that could put you on the road to "dealing" like a millionaire.

I told you at the beginning of this chapter that these confidential business loans were unusual and off beat, but they show you that people in all walks of life are seeking ways to increase their income by breaking out of the job routine to successful businesses of their own.

Well, now the money-getting power of borrowed money is yours. So, don't hold back if there is anything you ever wanted to do and lack of money was holding you back. Don't be modest, satisfy your every desire. The power of borrowed money can produce miracles for you.

A FASCINATING AND PECULIAR BUSINESS THAT CAN BRING YOU $200,000 ANNUALLY

Here is a remarkable ad that appeared in the financial section of a local newspaper.

"Too many investors spend their time and money, wishing for something to happen to make them rich." But you can make it happen. Attend our seminar on "How Not To Go Broke When Investing."

This was part of an advertisement requesting people who were interested in putting money in the stock market, to attend a one day meeting at a local hotel.

The fee was $75, which included meals and printed materials.

I have always been interested in any peculiar

business, so I went. When I arrived at the registration desk, would you believe that there were eighty people who had forked over $75 to attend the seminar, or rally, as some would call it.

It didn't take long to figure that eighty people at $75 a head was $6,000 for one day's work. We immediately set about to make acquaintance with Charles Gillmor, the entrepreneur who was sponsoring the event.

$$ How Charles G. Picks up $6,000
for a One Day Work Week

When the seminar was concluded, the hand-shaking was over, and the participants were leaving, all excited about their future and with a new plan of action on "how to invest their money," Charles invited me to his hotel room.

It was a fascinating experience as he related to me the potential amount of money that could be made conducting rallys or seminars.

My first question was why people would pay $75 to $1500, even paying their own travel expenses, for a one day or one week long seminar?

People, he said, want to hear experts talk on a subject that they are interested in. And, in addition, it gives them a chance to ask questions about the subject.

Many of the speakers at this rally had published books or reports on the subject, but people still wanted the information from the author. That is why Charles told me, they will pay for first-hand information, and feel they have received their money's worth.

HOW TO GET LARGE
CORPORATIONS TO
SUBSCRIBE TO YOUR SERVICE

Charles pointed out that large corporations are the biggest supporters of a seminar. It seems that at the executive level they can see the benefits for themselves as well as for key employees. And they are in a position to pay the fees for employees who attend.

A seminar or workshop covers a wide range of subjects, from "How to Be the World's Greatest Salesman" to "How to Raise Earthworms for a Profit."

Your rally or seminar should be directed to those who wish to improve their knowledge or skills to handle their jobs more efficiently.

Large corporations know that the employee who goes along day by day, without taking on new responsibilities, does not progress — and often the best employee gets into a rut. A seminar could be just the thing to inspire an employee to reach greater goals, which in turn, creates a greater output of services for the corporation.

Many businesses are eager to send employees to a workshop that is oriented to their business, if for nothing more than to get some of their key people away from their television set for an evening. They know that the prime requisite to a successful career is concentration of thought. Large corporations will be glad to pay you a fee to motivate their employees to greater action.

HOW TO GET EXPERTS TO
PROMOTE FOR YOU — FREE

Everyone is an expert in some field of business, and anyone outstanding in his own field has a healthy ego factor. You will find him as guest speaker at various clubs, the Lions, Rotary, anywhere he can get an invitation to speak. He is happy to give his lectures free. And, don't forget new authors are looking for ways to get their name before the public.

What better way than giving a FREE LECTURE at your workshop.

The beauty of a seminar is you don't have to know a thing on the subject matter. Let's say you are putting together a rally on the subject of "How to Make a Million Dollars Raising Rabbits."

You could find a dozen experts in your city who know the rabbit business. Simply extend an invitation for them to speak to a group of people who are interested in rabbits, and you have your experts eager to promote your rally — free.

One thing to keep in mind. If they have a book or a product related to the subject, they will approach you for the right to sell after the meetings. Fair enough. You have made your money up front by collecting fees from registered attendees.

HOW TO CONTACT 10,000 PROSPECTS EAGER TO PUT CASH IN YOUR BUSINESS

Let's say you have chosen a hot subject and made arrangements for speakers that people would like to hear. It is possible for you to draw from 100 to 300 people to your rally. And, if you figure $100 a head, simple arithmetic tells that you have $10,000 to $30,000 potential profit.

How can we get prospects eager to send us cash to put into our business of promoting a rally or workshop?

Simple, let's say you live in a town of 50,000 or more. You could run space advertising in your local paper just as Charles Gillmor, and you would pick up a few prospects, enough to make a profit. But the pros who deal like millionaires use rented mailing lists.

For example, you have decided to use the subject I mentioned previously, "How to Make a Million Dollars Raising Rabbits." You can rent a list of 10,000 prospects who are interested in your subject, locally and in surrounding towns.

Check your yellow pages under "Mailing List Rentals." Choosing your list broker is important. We have had great success with Dependable Lists, Inc., and Dunhill, of New York City. If they don't have a branch office in your area, give them a call. They will be eager to help you select prospects in your area on any subject you choose.

And that's not all. They will give you free counseling service on your mailing list package, with suggestions on how to get the greatest number of prospects from your rented list of 10,000 or any size list you wish to select. They have practical "How to" methods for the beginner that can literally transform your workshop into thousands of dollars in no time at all.

One suggestion, if you are unable to prepare your own invitation "mail package" to your potential prospects, spend the extra money to hire a good copywriter. Try to send out your invitations at least 90 days before the date of your workshop.

Let me tell you, right here, don't forget the telephone. If you have a list with 10,000 names or less, spend a few days calling your prospects. Explain the subject matter, and who the speakers will be. Get his opinion on the rally. It is possible to obtain a hundred participants for your rally over the phone.

It is a fascinating business. It works. Just watch your mail. Also, watch the space advertising in magazines, all inviting you to a rally or seminar. It's big money just waiting for you to organize your own seminar or workshop. You could become a millionaire in a few years, starting with no cash.

$$ How George F. Receives 70% of Gross Receipts — Never Leaves His Office

Practically any topic can be promoted to the mass market. Knowing this, George F., an insurance agent, regularly promotes one or two rallys a year, never leaves his office, and receives 70% of the gross receipts. In fact, he does none of the work, he hires experts. There are a few companies that do nothing but organize workshops for other people for a fee, usually 10% to 30% of gross receipts, depending on the amount of leg work and the number attending the rally.

If you would like to learn more about this angle of seminars, you can check out the yellow pages again. Look under the heading "Seminar Producers" or similar headings. Incidentally, the majority of seminar producers are located in New York.

Can the fascinating and peculiar business of rallys change your life? You bet it can — to the tune of thousands of dollars a year if you promote it right. It could be the best investment in your future wealth and happiness that you ever made. Millions of dollars are being made in rallys every year by people like you, so why not join those who are "dealing" like millionaires in seminars.

HOW TO COMPETE WITH COMPETITION AND TAKE HOME THE PROFITS

I would be short-changing you if I didn't mention competition.

I have in mind a small grocery store, that for several years had its own way and sold a hundred thousand dollars worth of merchandise a year. Then a supermarket moved in across the street as his major competitor. This woke up the owner, and today his store does five times the business it did before his competitor moved in.

This should tell us one thing. Don't worry about the competition. Try to get as much good as possible from them.

If your competition comes up with a good idea, don't knock it. Copy it! Get in on the benefits and try to better it with your own ideas. Then you will take home more profits in your own business.

Remember the days of "gas wars"? It seemed price cutting was the way to get advantage over your competitors. Don't follow the leader, but look for ways to improve your service. Find ways to give your customer quality and quantity for the same money. Remember, if you increase value for the dollar, you will find it will be easier to make a dollar.

More dollars mean more profits to take home.

That is why you should view your competitor as the pacesetter, not someone who is out to steal your business.

If you hired two top consultants to study your business and recommend improvements, you would probably benefit, but not enough to pay the high fee they would demand. But, if you had two competitors in your town, who are burning midnight oil on ways to improve their business, you can get the benefit of their thinking, and it doesn't cost you a cent.

Get busy. Compete with your competitors and take home the profits like a millionaire.

CHAPTER EIGHT

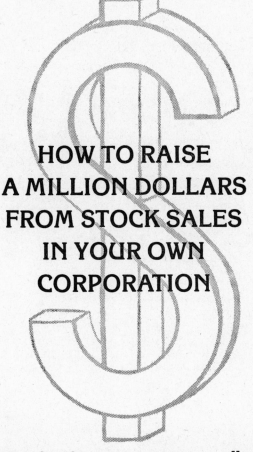

HOW TO RAISE
A MILLION DOLLARS
FROM STOCK SALES
IN YOUR OWN
CORPORATION

The very idea that you can raise a million dollars from your own stock sales may seem far fetched, but it can be done. Millions of dollars are raised every day from this source, and I believe you can do the same thing.

The steps you must take are outlined for you in this chapter. However, if your company has no business "track record," but you can prove the potential, you can take the route of raising money by selling stock in your own corporation.

First you must comply with the rules of the Securities and Exchange Commission and your own state laws dealing with the sale of securities. Then there may be local regulations that must be satisfied, but you can do it.

$$ How Jimmy L. Sold Stock at State Fairs, and Now Has One of the Largest Corporations in His State

You have probably heard of Ling-Tempco-Vought, one of the fifty largest corporations in the United States.

Jimmy Ling, a former electrician, lived in the state of Texas and was the founder of Ling-Tempco-Vought. He formed his corporation under the state laws of Texas, received his clearance from the SEC, and complied with all local laws.

When the State Fair of Texas opened that year, Mr. Ling rented a booth and sold shares in his corporation. So, it can be done.

However, before you rush out and rent space at a fair, there are a few things you should know about the kind of stock you are going to offer to the public.

First, let me say I am not advising on securities nor giving legal advice. Always get current professional help. This chapter is written to furnish you with guidelines on how you can raise capital from stock sales in your own corporation.

There are five basic types of securities:

1. *Common Stock*
2. *Preferred Stock*
3. *Debentures*
4. *Indentures*
5. *Bonds*

To select the type of securities you plan to sell to the public, let's look at each one as a layman, then pick the one that is most practical for your corporation.

First: Common stock — The majority of investors understand this type of security. They know they are buying shares in a company and expect to share in the profits through dividends. And, if the stock is ever traded, they could expect a gain in value.

If you are planning to sell to the general public, common stock could possibly be your most successful route.

Second: Preferred Stock — is for the person who doesn't enjoy a risk. Most generally, preferred stock has a guaranteed percent return. (In other words, no dividend can be paid on common stock until all dividends on preferred stock are satisfied.)

Third: Debentures — are promissory notes secured by the good credit and assets of the company, and usually not backed by mortgages.

Fourth: Indenture Bonds — are usually secured by the physical properties of the company. If you plan to buy real estate or equipment for your business, indenture bonds wouldn't be wise.

Fifth: Bonds — They can be corporate, municipal or government. They have a face value and a stipulated interest rate and maturity date.

HOW TO PUT A SWEETENER IN YOUR BOND ISSUE AN INVESTOR CAN'T REFUSE

The important thing to remember here is that small investors are sometimes slow to invest in bonds. They may be scared off by the long maturity dates, some as long as thirty years. However, bonds can be sold before the maturity date to overcome the inertia of the hesitant purchaser, and you could sweeten the pot with what is known as a "convertible option".

The bond owner can collect his stipulated interest while he observes the progress of your company.

And, when he wishes, he can convert his bond into common or preferred stock.

With the convertible feature to your bond, your investor can have his cake and eat it too. It takes out the fear of risk and he gets a chance to share in your success.

But that's not all. Don't overlook the warrants that you can attach to your bonds. These are simply an option to buy stock in your company at a certain price, within a given period of time. Warrants are used by large corporations as inducements to buy. Why not use them, also, as you begin to raise a million dollars from stock sales in your own company.

The selling of a bond issue would probably be the most difficult to get off the ground, because most investors are guided by ratings of bonds.

For instance, Standard and Poors rate bonds as follows:

AAA The highest grade — The ultimate in protection

 AA High grade, but lower quality

  A Better medium grade, with good investment strength

BBB Medium grade — Suspect to business conditions

 BB Has possibilities, but low earnings

  B Speculative — Payments of interest not assured

CCC Highly speculative

 CC Highly speculative

We can see the problems we would encounter if we tried to float a bond issue, but millions are raised through bond issues. Don't rule them out completely.

If you plan to sell securities in your own corporation, common stock would be the best and easiest to sell. You would receive the least resistance from the investing public. They understand stocks, so you don't have to explain all the technical terms of debentures, yields, convertibles, coupons and other data that would only scare off potential buyers.

Before you launch your campaign to sell stock in your company, discuss the plan with your attorney and tax accountant. You may save dollars and time. And, don't forget to consult your banker — get expert advice.

Once you have decided to raise money through stock sales, your first step would be to notify the Securities and Exchange Commission about filing your offer.

For instance, if you plan to sell stock only to local residents or investors in your state, for not over half a million dollars, the SEC doesn't require you to file (subject to change). But, if some of your stockholders sell their stock to someone out of your state within a year, they would require you to file an application with the SEC. It would be well if you had some type of agreement with each buyer, that he would hold his stock for twelve months from date of purchase. Then you would only be required to notify the SEC of the intended sale of stock.

HOW TO RAISE $50,000 CASH IMMEDIATELY — WITHOUT FILING A PROSPECTUS WITH SEC

Here is an astonishing way to raise money, if you only need $50,000 to keep your business on a paying basis. Here is a method that you can use to sell stocks that doesn't require you to file with the SEC. However, you must notify them of the pending sale.

This is known as Rule 257. (You can obtain all the details from the Securities and Exchange Commission.) This route is open only to existing businesses — not new enterprises.

To sell under Rule 257, you must have a good earning record and a good performance record. But, it is an easy and simple way to raise $50,000 without a set date to repay.

However, if you want to roll up your sleeves and really hit the jackpot, why not fill out the paperwork, file with the SEC, and try for half a million dollars. This method of raising money is known as "Regulation A," and is rather simple.

The forms are not difficult to fill out. You simply tell who you are and the kind of securities you intend to sell to the public.

There is one requirement. You must file your intent at least ten days before the date of sale.

The SEC will send you a letter that will either give you a "Stopaction" or a go ahead. One word of caution — even if you are given the green light, the SEC reserves the right to stop sales on a moment's notice. And the kicker, if your offer isn't valid, you must refund all monies and file a complete and full report before sales may be resumed.

Please remember, in your efforts to "deal" like a millionaire, you must never resort to fraud. So in all cases, when filing your prospectus with the SEC, tell the plain and simple truth. There are a lot of people in jail because of stock frauds. You are interested in making a lot of money — not in serving time in the "bar hotel."

If you are filing under "Regulation A," you must state that you are a new company and there is no earnings record. This will not affect your stock sales. Most investors in a new company know there is no performance record, but are looking for a ground floor opportunity to get rich. They know there is an element of risk in any new business, and they know the great potential of a sound business under good management.

So, that is why you don't have to make false or wild claims that you can't lose or that you can double your money in a few days.

Tell the truth, the whole truth and nothing but the truth, and you will raise hundreds of thousands of dollars from your own corporate stock sales. I flatly believe that if you put your mind to it, you can raise a million dollars from stock sales in your own company.

HOW TO SELL ALL YOUR
SHARES OF STOCK BEFORE
GOING PUBLIC

In Chapter 6 "How Millionaires Raise Money for New Ideas", I mentioned that there are more people looking for ways to invest money than there were sound money — making ideas available. That is why many investors turn to stocks. But that is not all — many people with money to invest are fully convinced that stocks are the only investments available.

This provides us with a simple method to sell stock, and you don't need to notify the SEC. It is known as the "Private Sale" of stock to a select group.

For example, if you can select a group of people with the same interests, such as doctors, dentists, or another professional group who have something in common and are willing to invest in your enterprise, you would have a private offering — not a public sale. One word of caution. If you need ten investors, and have to offer 200 prospects to sell ten investors, you are going public, and the SEC could require a filing. Your best bet is to hold a meeting, with special written invitations to your prospects, then you will have an opportunity to explain your program.

In addition, don't overlook seminars. In Chapter 7, I mentioned a seminar I attended, where I paid $75 as a registration fee. Why not use the reverse twist. Advertise a *free seminar* on investing in your type of industry.

You could contact some influential person in your community, your banker or attorney, to give a lecture on your type of business. He wouldn't try to sell stock in your company, but could list the great potential in your type of business. After the meeting, hand out your prospectus or literature explaining your stock offer.

Don't overlook this important point. When your speaker is introduced, mention he is sponsored by the XYZ Company, your corporation. Also, make sure that everyone who attends signs the guest book with name, address and telephone number. This gives you a prospect list. You can use it at a later date to sell your stock.

The seminar adds a little zest and enthusiasm to your type of business. Don't overlook the free refreshments. People enjoy visiting over drinks, while discussing your money-making proposition.

A CLOSELY GUARDED CAMPAIGN
THAT COULD RAISE A MILLION
DOLLARS FOR YOU —
ALMOST OVERNIGHT

You may be well on your way to bringing in more cash to your company than you ever dreamed possible in such a short time. When you decide you are going to sell stock in your corporation, don't overlook a closely guarded campaign that begins with the officers of the company. You can't run an ad in the newspaper for salesmen, or recruit women to sell house to house. The secret is in how you divide up the sales among the officers of your corporation.

Remember, selling stock is like selling anything else. You must prepare, develop a sales pitch, advertise and train personnel. If you have a friend who is a stock broker, you could have him recruit security sales people for your campaign on a commission basis.

If you wish to save the expense of security salesmen, then we must proceed with the officers of the company.

To sell stock in your new corporation, with no record of earnings, will require a larger number of prospects for each officer than if your company was nationally known.

However, you have a big plus in your favor. All officers and directors can contact all their friends and relatives. This is the first step used by all new salesmen, regardless of the product. This accounts for the large turnover rate among new salesmen. As soon as they run out of friends and relatives, they quit or hunt for another product and start all over again.

Before you spend any money on your sales campaign, contact your attorney to make sure all your forms, your prospectus and sales materials are legal. For additional protection, visit your regional SEC office. They will be glad to offer suggestions and point out areas that will need changing.

Regulations governing sale of stock issues are constantly changing. Get all the information you can, then launch your campaign among friends and relatives. It is possible to sell at least half of your issue in a few days. You can see for yourself how easy it is to raise thousands of dollars from a "Private Sale" of your corporate stock.

HOW TO FIND STOCK BUYERS
READY FOR INSTANT PURCHASE
THAT WILL PUT THOUSANDS
OF DOLLARS IN YOUR COMPANY

Let's say your goal is $100,000 and you have sold half of your issue to friends and relatives. This leaves $50,000 that you must sell to what is known as "cold prospects."

First, consult the yellow pages of your phone book. Make a list of all the professional men in your city. They are to be contacted by telephone, or are mailed a copy of your prospectus.

Incidentally, your mailing package should consist of a copy of your approval from the SEC, plus any letters from prominent people who will give recommendations for your company. You should include a brief personal history of the officers and directors, along with the projected growth of your company.

At this point, you can make use of your bank. Let them be the transfer agent of all stock purchases. They will be glad to handle it, if all money collected is deposited in their bank.

Our next source of "cold prospects" is rented names. You contact a mailing list broker who can get you a list of investors in your area. As mentioned, I have had great success with Dependable Lists, Inc., of New York. Also, if you would like an unending list of brokers, plus a classification of mail order purchasers of stocks, write Direct Mail Lists, Rates And Data, 5201 Old Orchard Road, Skokie, Illinois 60076, for their subscription rates.

Once you have a copy of your list of investors, it gives you everything you need. Break the list down into towns, then you can begin your telephone campaign. The rented lists don't have telephone numbers, but you can look them up and transfer to 3 x 5 index cards.

Be sure to keep a total of buyers from each rented list. If one list produces more potential buyers than another, you will be able to order more names from that list broker in case you need more prospects.

If you have ever worked in a "boiler room" type of phone solicitation, you know the sales people have a canned sales pitch, and they work on the law of averages.

You may prefer not to use the same type of operation for your stock sales pitch, but you must have a well defined presentation.

First, you are talking to people who have money to invest, and know a little about common stocks. You should know some of the securities lingo to carry on an intelligent conversation. (I have included a valuable glossary of investment terms at the conclusion of this chapter. You can't learn them all, but pick out a few words to use in your sales presentation.)

You have one point in your favor. The prospect is interested in speculation, and you must convince him of the growth potential of your company. Don't get involved in side issues, such as P & E ratios, warrants and debentures. Stick to your big guns — the growth and sound management policy of your company. Convince him that your stock will increase in price as your company grows, and you will get a good-sized check from the prospect in the mail.

And in addition, don't overlook the individual who is a stock collector. This type of prospect very seldom sells his stock. He likes to tie his certificates in little bundles and stash them in a safety deposit box at his bank. He collects stock like a stamp collector collects stamps.

You will find this type of investor interested in dividends, so tailor your presentation to the dividend angle. Let him know he is going to share in the profit of your company.

Here is an inside tip given to me by a security salesman. If you are selling to a businessman who could supply you with merchandise, it is good to mention that you could possibly use their goods and services. You don't make a deal to that effect, but you could leave the impression that management is look-

ing for his type of service. He understands there is a
possibility of a profit in the stock purchase and he
may also become one of the principal suppliers.

You will be surprised at the number of people
who will be eager to put money in a good solid growth
company. There are people with thousands of dollars,
waiting to buy shares in your corporation.

HOW YOU OBTAIN INSTANT PUBLICITY IN THE FINANCIAL COMMUNITY

As I mentioned, selling is telling, and telling is
advertising. But please remember, the SEC takes a
dim view of any flowery methods of advertising. In
fact, it limits your advertising to your name and the
offering, and an invitation to send for your prospectus.

Pick up a *Forbes* magazine or a copy of the *Wall
Street Journal* and check out some of the display ads.
This will give you an idea on how your own ad should
be written if you decide to use the print media.

You are interested in how to let people in your
local financial community know that you have stock
available. It is simple — you let someone else do the
leg work.

For instance, Ralph N., a mechanic without any
working knowledge of public relations, simply hired
a local public relations firm. He had them set up a
public relations campaign by holding an open house
at his new auto tune-up center. They made arrangements for a ribbon cutting ceremony to open his
place of business. The local newspaper reporter was
there, along with some prominent local city council-
men. He provided plenty of "freebies" for everyone
present — coffee, cake and balloons for the kids with
his company name printed on each one.

He then arranged for one of the officers of the
corporation to volunteer to lecture at all the local

civic clubs. Try to follow up as soon as possible after the "grand opening."

The idea is to get your company name before all the prospects possible. It will be much easier to sell your stock now that you have become well known in the local financial community.

You may say at this point, "That costs money." You are right, but keep in mind that you are raising capital to put you on the road to being "well fixed" for life right in your own town.

A successful stock campaign could be the best way to put you on the road to "dealing" like a millionaire.

A FINGER TIP INVESTMENT GLOSSARY THAT MAKES YOU A FINANCIAL EXPERT

Average: The best known is the Dow-Jones Industrial Average, which plots price changes of thirty industrial stocks. Prices of the stocks in the "Dow" are not divided by thirty to get the average, but by 1.71 to provide continuity after many stock splits and stock dividends.

Bear market: A period of declining prices.

Bearer bond: A bond which does not have the owner's name recorded.

Blue chip: Stock of an investment-grade company of the highest standing.

Bond: The evidence of a corporate, municipal, or government debt, expressed in a stipulated face value, a stipulated rate of interest, and a date at which the issuer will pay the holder the face value of the bond.

Bull market: A period of rising prices.

Capital gain or loss: Profit or loss from the sale of an asset, recognized by the tax laws as differing in kind from profit or loss from the asset's use.

Cash flow: The difference between what a company takes in for sales and services and what it lays out in expenses, taxes, and other costs that must be met immediately.

Collateral: Property pledged by a borrower to secure repayment of a loan.

Commission: The broker's fee for buying or selling securities.

Common stock: The shares representing the ownership of a corporation.

Dealer: A buyer and seller of securities who maintains an inventory of the issues in which he trades.

Debenture: A promissory note secured only by the general credit and assets of a company.

Depreciation: A charge against earnings to compensate for the limited useful lives of plant and machinery.

Dollar averaging: A system of buying stocks at regular intervals. A fixed amount regularly invested buys more shares in a low market and fewer in a high market. When averaged over a long term, a relatively low price per share results.

Face value: The amount of the promise to pay.

Fiscal year: A corporation's accounting year.

Fixed charges: Expenses such as bond interest, taxes and royalties, which a company must meet whether it has earnings or not.

General mortgage bond: A bond secured by a blanket mortgage on a corporation's property.

Hedging: Protecting oneself against wide market swings by taking both buy and sell positions in a security.

Investment banker: The middleman between the corporation that wants to raise money and the public.

Investment trust: A company that invests in other companies after which it sells its own shares to the public.

Leverage: The practice of putting a larger sum than one has in hand at risk by using margin loans, warrants, or puts and calls.

Liquidity: The degree of ease with which a security can be converted into cash.

Open order: An order to buy stock, valid until it is executed or countermanded.

Par value: For a stock, the dollar amount assigned each share of stock in the company's charter.

Point: For a stock, $1 in price; for a bond, $10 in price.

Price-earnings ratio: Current market price of a stock dividend by twelve-month earnings per share.

Profit margin: A measure of earning capacity after taxes.

Prospectus: A circular that describes securities being offered for sale. The prospectus is required by the Securities Act of 1933.

Proxy: Written authorization permitting someone else to vote a stockholder's shares.

Rights: When a company issues additional stock, it often gives its stockholders rights to buy the new shares ahead of other buyers in proportion to the number of shares each owns.

Tax-exempt bond: A bond which pays no Federal taxes because it is issued by a state or a subordinate division of a state.

Transfer agent: The institution that keep a record of each stockholder, his address, and the number of shares he owns.

Warrant: A paper giving its holder the right to buy a security at a set price, either within a specified period or perpetually.

CHAPTER NINE

HOW TO SELL
A MILLION DOLLARS WORTH
OF REAL ESTATE
USING INSIDE SECRETS
OF MONEY LENDERS

The inside information in this chapter is based on my own personal experience, gained after serving twenty-five years on loan committees and Boards of Directors of various lending institutions. What you read isn't information you can obtain at a school, or something that wishful thinking can bring about. These are facts which have helped me accumulate wealth in the real estate profession that I didn't dream possible a few years ago.

After you have finished reading this chapter, I

am confident that you will see how the knowledge gained is going to increase your income, which, in turn, will greatly increase your net worth.

The first part of this chapter will acquaint you with the inside information that is used by loan committees to set standards for the approval or rejection of a loan you have submitted for a buyer of a home.

The second portion of the chapter explains a secret *"Three Word Formula"* that enables you to qualify a prospect for a home loan, even before he tours your "open house."

The final section contains little known secrets on how to obtain listings that few real estate people know or will ever learn of in a lifetime.

There is a bonus section on "Why people buy homes". This information will increase your income beyond your expectations.

HOW YOU CAN COLLECT HUGE COMMISSIONS FOR YOUR SERVICES

Have you ever asked the question, "Why can a doctor collect more for his services than a day laborer?" The answer is: Special knowledge, judgment and skill. His patients pay the price because they don't want to run the risk of treating themselves or taking the advice of well-meaning friends or relatives.

Why can a lawyer collect large fees for his services? For the same reason — he has special knowledge, judgment and skill. His clients come to him because they want expert legal advice from a person they can trust.

Now, ask yourself, "What do I know about real estate that the average businessman doesn't know?" Do you have the special knowledge, judgment and skill to work out real estate problems which your friends and relatives don't possess? If you do, those who wish to buy or sell a house will be glad to pay you a liberal price to handle their transactions.

You and I know there are many people trying to buy or sell homes on the advice of their friends or relatives, and they wouldn't think of trusting them if they needed a doctor or a lawyer. The first step in your town or city is to let people know that you are a professional. They should come to you with their real estate problems.

This chapter is one more tool to help you to be more successful and to collect more money as you solve the problems people encounter in buying and selling their property. I would like to repeat something that you and I have heard many times, "Honesty is the best policy". How true this is in real estate. We have seen many men lose a sale by being evasive or just plain untruthful to questions asked by their prospective buyers. We have always made it a point to tell a customer the truth, and it is with the same policy that I give you the information contained in this chapter.

We have tried not to include any impractical information or use terms in the lending industry that you may not be familiar with. At the end of this chapter, there is included a glossary of "lending terms" for your use in talking to a loan officer, which we will discuss in greater detail later. Don't try to learn all of them, for I doubt if a loan officer knows them all, but we have circled a few words which will benefit you in any discussion with anyone on a loan committee.

HOW TO SPOT THE KEY MAN IN A LENDING INSTITUTION THAT COULD LOAN YOU MILLIONS

To begin to use the inside information contained in this chapter, we would first like to acquaint you with the "Authority Chain" in a lending institution. There may be a difference in various banks and savings and loan associations, but they are basically alike and serve the same purpose. Please note the "Authority Chart" which I have prepared for you.

Don't panic at all the headings listed. There is only one you should remember, and that is the Mortgage Officer (Key Man), which is circled on the chart. He is going to be the key to your success.

I will go more into detail concerning the mortgage officer, whom I will refer to from now on as the "Loan Officer," later in this chapter. He is of utmost concern, for it is his prime responsibility to make loans for his company which will increase their earnings.

The Board of Directors at the top of the Authority Chain is not of major concern. True, they have the responsibility for the overall operation of the lending institution, but they seldom see the loan application you have submitted to your loan officer. They usually ratify or approve the loans after they have been closed and you have received the money on your house sale. The primary function of the Board of Directors is to set goals, policies, and procedures for management to follow in the day-to-day operations of the lending institution.

Now, notice on the "Authority Chart", beneath the Board of Directors you will find the Loan Committee. These are the men and women who make the loan decisions — whether to approve or reject the buyer your loan officer has submitted to them. They have the information obtained from your customer, credit reports, appraisals, and other data required to make sound decisions. From the loan committee's meeting comes the decision on whether you sell a home or lose a sale. If approved, the committee makes a commitment to close the loan for you. After contacting your buyer, a time is set for closing, and you have a happy home owner plus a nice profit for your

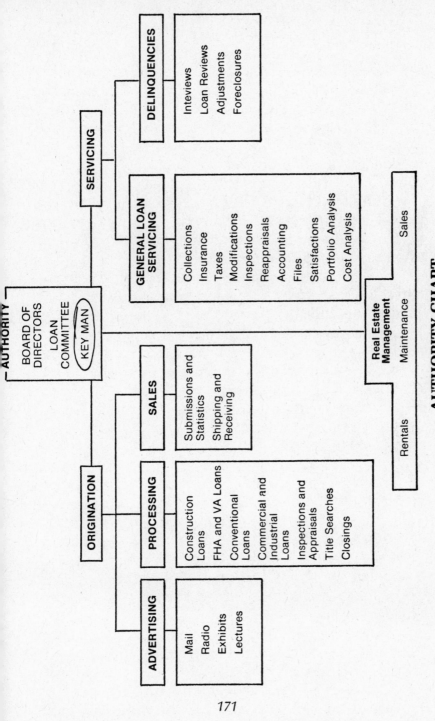

AUTHORITY CHART

professional services. If the loan is rejected, you lose
a sale.

Here is where I would like to mention that members of the loan committee are human. At times they
reject a buyer for lack of information, or the individual just doesn't qualify. I have sat in on many loan
committee meetings and have observed that one day
the members may approve a loan and on the next day
they would reject the same customer.

Why? They are human and often under various
pressures. They have daily problems themselves, and
at times will hurry through an application, which
often results in a reject. Possibly the Chairman is late
for his golf game, so your loan customer doesn't receive his just dues. My reference to this is not intended to point a finger at the loan committee,
because I have seen them bend over backwards to get
a buyer approved. But, if your customer "died in committee," you need someone to champion your cause.

Early in this chapter, I pointed out that there was
chiefly one person to be concerned with — *the loan
officer*. He is your key man.

Looking at the chart, you will see a line drawn
down to "Real Estate Management," and to the right,
"Sales." This is what you are interested in, because in
real estate, this is where you make your money —
sales.

The loan officer is your direct contact to the authority that approves or disapproves your customer,
the loan committee. The loan officer is usually a *member* of the loan committee. From this, you can see why
he is our "key."

Stop for a moment and ask yourself this question,
"Is the loan officer I am presently doing business with
a *member* of the loan committee?" This is important,
for it is a fact that not all loan officers have a seat on
the committee. If the answer to your question is, "I
don't know," the first thing tomorrow, call him on the

phone and ask him. If he says, "No," keep him as a coffee drinking buddy, but find out which loan officer is on the loan committee. You should get to be on a first name basis with him, and then see that he gets all your future loan applications, for he is the one who will champion your cause during loan meetings.

For instance, during a meeting, he will usually be asked by other committee members why he recommends your customer for a loan, and if he has done his homework, he will enthusiastically defend your customer's right to be approved.

Keep this in mind — the loan officer must make loans to keep his job. Also, he may be striving for a seat on the Board of Directors. So, by all means, make sure your loan officer is a member of the loan committee.

HOW THE CREDIT ANALYSIS
OF A PROSPECT PUTS
DOLLARS IN YOUR POCKET

Shortly after leaving the banking and lending industry, I attended one of the finest real estate colleges in Oklahoma City. I was amazed that there wasn't a course on "How to Qualify a Prospect for a Home Loan."

To further understand the functions of your loan officer and loan committee, you need some insight on how they analyze the credit worthiness of your buyer. As mentioned, we are going to give you a secret "Three Word Formula" through which, in only a few minutes of conversation with a prospect, you can obtain enough information to know if he can qualify for a home loan. If he can't qualify, you wouldn't want to waste your time trying to sell him a house.

Please don't turn to the end of this chapter to find the "Three Word Formula", for at this point you wouldn't understand how to put the information to profitable use. Believe me, it works! As soon as I received my real estate license, I went to work for a broker who sent me into a new addition he had developed. By using the formula, along with the other information in this chapter, I sold thirty-five new houses, while my competitor friend in the same addition sold six. It wasn't because I was the best salesman. I simply used banking and lending principles mentally to qualify a prospect.

This is what I want you to do. It means many more sales than you ever thought possible.

The first concern of a loan officer is whether the customer will be able to meet the payments on his new purchase. Let's face it, if no buyer ever defaulted on a mortgage, there would never be any risk in making a home loan. People vary in their attitudes toward paying their debts and the amount of house payment they can assume. This is learned through a credit check, but the amount of payment per month, in addition to taxes and insurance on the home, is of primary concern to your loan officer. Also, utilities are taken into consideration. Taxes, insurance, and utilities must be added to the monthly payment to determine the basic amount the customer can afford to spend each month out of his income for mortgage payments.

There is always a full credit investigation of your customer because the lender expects to have him as a customer for many years. A foreclosure is expensive to a lender and customer. Only when the customer keeps paying can the lender make money. This is why a loan committee is more concerned with the good paying habits of your customer than the appraised value of a house. Here we can use an old army expression, "First line of defense".

The first line of defense against a loss for a lender is the ability and willingness of a homeowner to pay. If a loan officer could approve loans that never defaulted, he wouldn't need a second line of defense.

This is impossible to do. There are too many unforeseen events that can happen during the life of a loan. There can be illness, loss of income, even death. With unforeseen events as a possible hazard, the loan officer must have a second line of defense or protection for his loan.

Here is where the mortgage comes in, and at this stage, they just hope their appraisal was as accurate as possible, so the lender won't sustain a loss.

Next, the lender has a third line of defense which is seldom used. If there is a deficiency balance, does the customer have the assets to overcome the loss and can they legally be attached? You can be comforted with this fact: during my twenty-five years in the banking and lending industry, I can count on my fingers the number of times I had to use the third line of defense, which proves that the majority of buyers want to meet their mortgage payments.

You must never forget that the loan officer is not only a friend of yours, he becomes a friend to your prospect. He knows that the customer is anxious to move into his new home. The mother is concerned about enrolling the children in school. The children are wondering what the "kids" in the new neighborhood are like.

It may be the biggest financial obligation your customer ever makes in a lifetime when he signs a contract to buy a house you have suggested from your listings.

Your loan officer doesn't want this family to fail in its new venture. It is his duty as a loan officer to point out, if necessary, the fallacy of buying a home that the individual cannot afford, which would be a burdensome load over the years, or might even lead to foreclosure and the loss of his home. This would lead to a bad experience, not only for the family, but also for the lender.

If the loan officer rejects a loan because the cus-

tomer's income isn't sufficient to meet the monthly
payment on the house he selected, he can help you
match a house to the monthly payment your customer
can meet. Get his suggestions, because lenders are
placing more emphasis on the ability of a customer to
meet future payments. The appraisal of a house is
becoming less and less important.

Keep this in mind, for it will help in qualifying a
customer for a home loan.

INSIDE INFORMATION FROM
CREDIT REPORTS THAT CAN
SKYROCKET YOUR SALES

"Factual" and "intangible" are the types of information gathered for a credit analysis. "Factual"
is the information that can be verified direct, such as:
income, employment, how long on job, and position.

"Intangible" concerns a person's living habits,
marital relationship and social habits — does he
drink and so on.

The first item a loan officer examines on a loan
application is the income and employment. This is his
gauge for the ability and stability of the prospect you
have submitted for a loan. There is a rule of thumb he
goes by. For example, a family can usually afford a
home costing two and a half times its annual income.
Here is a simpler rule: *One week's salary equals one
monthly payment.* If you know the monthly payments
on your houses, then it is easy to know how expensive
a home the prospect can afford once you determine
his weekly pay.

There is one fact I observed while serving on
loan committees which has been extremely beneficial and has helped me to successfully sell real
estate — almost 99 out of 100 *previous home owners*
were approved for another home loan, whereas the
majority of rejects were those trying to buy a home
for the first time.

The employment of a prospect should show he has been in the same line of work for at least *three years*. If a prospect has a history of *job-hopping* due to his inability to keep a job, he will rate *very low* on approval. However, if the history shows that he changed jobs several times in the same line of work for more money or better position, it shows he is ambitious, and his rating will be very high. On the other hand, permanent employees on the same jobs for several years contribute to the *stability factor* and are usually approved if all other information is favorable.

"A man's word is his bond." How true this quotation is in the lending business. A person with a bad credit record and job-hopping isn't considered a good loan risk.

There are many ways to find out the paying habits of a customer. The local credit bureau is most commonly used. Some firms use only direct calls to references or written letters for the information. The credit paying habits of a customer play a major part in what action is taken by a loan officer. There is a saying among loan officers that "A person with good paying habits doesn't go bad overnight", and by the same token, "A person with bad paying habits doesn't have a change of heart overnight and start paying everybody he owes".

There are many, many factors taken into consideration in approving loans, but if your loan officer is a member of a loan committee, you can be assured he has the proven judgment and the ability to handle your customer's loan application. He will have the best interests of your customer in mind, and at the same time, the safety of the lender's money.

At the beginning of this chapter, we promised you a "Three Word Formula" on how to qualify a prospect for a loan. Study this until it becomes a part of your sales presentation automatically. After the first time you use this, you will mentally see the great benefits it is going to bring to you in future home sales.

THREE SECRET WORDS THAT
WILL QUALIFY YOUR PROSPECT
FOR A LOAN: — ABILITY
— STABILITY — WILLINGNESS

These three words are going to save you many hours of trying to sell a prospect a house when he would never qualify for a home loan. The use of this formula is going to free you for more time with people who will qualify for a home loan, which, in turn, will mean more sales and more money.

You will need to have a ready reference to these words. You should keep them written in your notebook or use a 3 x 5 inch index card to carry in your pocket or handbag. Under *each word*, you will write down pertinent information to help you remember what to ask a person in order to obtain the information required to decide if a prospect can qualify for a home loan.

Ability

One week's pay equals one monthly payment!

If you have a customer whose income is *$250 a week*, you know he can qualify for a loan with a monthly payment of approximately *$250 per month*. Always make it a practice to have a ready reference of the monthly payments on every home you have listed. The moment you learn the weekly income of a prospect, you know what price range he can afford in a home. Then you show him houses in this price class, and for some strange reason, it is almost always one of these he purchases. It could be that the customer, himself, knows approximately what he can afford each month for house payments.

Also, you know that if a person earns $500.00 per week, he wouldn't be satisfied with a house with payments of $250.00 a month. You would simply check the houses that you have listed with payments of approximately $500.00 per month and recommend these to your customer.

Believe me, this system works. I have sold a million dollars' worth of real estate and have earned a lot of money using the system. I have also saved many hours of chauffeuring people around who wouldn't qualify for a home loan, if they insisted on buying a home with payments running over their weekly income.

Stability

Your customer should be in the same line of work for at least three years. Notice — *not the same job, but the same type* of work. If he changes jobs frequently, it should be the same work that he knows how to perform. Loan committees take a dim view of persons who go from job to job with no apparent reason.

For example, say a man worked for 10 years as a draftsman and now he has been an insurance salesman for two months. His chances for survival in the insurance business are slim, and his stability to repay a 30-year mortgage is even less.

Willingness

You can't look at a man and tell if he has a good paying record. But, I can tell you from many years' experience as a loan officer, no matter how much he makes or how many years he has been on the job, if his *willingness to repay his debts is bad*, the loan committee is going to turn him down for a home loan.

Now, here is the question — How can I tell if a prospect has good credit? There is no foolproof way without a credit investigation. However, there are a few signs to look for.

During your conversation with a customer, ask questions in an effort to qualify him in your mind for a home loan. Never hesitate to ask, "Have you ever been bankrupt?" You may think this would embarrass your customer and you would lose the sale. The opposite is true. I have never lost a customer by making this inquiry. You can rest assured that your loan officer is going to ask him, so you may as well get the information. If he says "yes," you are wasting your time trying to get him approved for a loan, unless he can justify his bankruptcy. I have seen very few in twenty-five years who could do so effectively enough to qualify for a loan.

If your customer says "no" to the question, he will usually begin to tell you his good credit references, because he is proud of his good paying record. He wants you to know he isn't a deadbeat.

You will also notice that a person who has *bad credit* will be *quick to sign a contract* just hoping that his home loan will be approved. If this is the case, you should get his name, address, and place of employment and telephone your loan officer. He can get a "quickie" credit report while you take your customer to coffee. It could save you several hours. If the report comes in "as agreed," you can proceed with your sale. If not, you can thank your customer for his time and proceed to more profitable prospects.

As mentioned, you need a ready reference notebook or a 3 x 5 index card. If you use a card, it should read like this:

> **ABILITY:**
> One week's income equals monthly payment.
> **STABILITY:**
> At least 3 years same line of work.
> **WILLINGNESS:**
> Have you ever been bankrupt?

You may wish to use more information for your notes. If so, please do. This should be read every morning before going to the office or before each appointment with a prospect. Make this a part of your sales approach. It will soon become second nature to you. You are going to be amazed when you see this simple "Three Word Formula" going to work for you.

I am now going to share some information on which *you cannot set a price* if you make it work. I have never given out this information to anyone else before now, and I am sure your loan officer may not approve of what I am going to tell you.

It began the day I sold my first house and had my purchase contract signed. My broker told me to take my customer and contract to the savings and loan association, where the loan officer would interview my customer to obtain a loan application. We all knew this took a lot of time. We had to drive across Oklahoma City and then endure a long wait in the lender's office. While waiting, I wondered why I couldn't take the loan application myself and phone it to the lender. I always have a small seat desk in my auto and could take down the information from the customer myself. This would not only save time, but wouldn't the customer rather give me the credit information, since at this point he considers me a friend? He would feel more relaxed with me, while with the loan officer, he is inclined to be ill at ease.

When I returned my customer back across town to the office, I telephoned the loan officer and explained that I had many years experience in taking loan applications, and if he would give me a pad of blank applications, I could interview my own customers and call in the information after they left the office. He not only said "yes", but brought me a pad of applications. I can now service three customers in the time it would normally take to service one.

You may be thinking that you don't have the experience necessary to fill out loan applications. This may be true, but if you can fill out listing blanks and sales contracts, you will have no problem with a loan application.

At this point, you have learned much of what your loan officer knows, and you can familiarize yourself with some of the words in the *glossary* at the end of this chapter. Then, when you talk to your loan officer, he may think you are an expert at taking applications.

The first opportunity you get, pick up the telephone and ask your loan officer for a pad of applications. He may just say, "Come by and pick them up." If he says "no", keep trying each time you see him. He just might bend the rules. After all, he is interested in more business, and this is a way to get it. Keep trying.

However, it may be that you would prefer taking your customer to the lender for the interview. I have taken only one, my first sale, and yet I have sold millions of dollars of real estate in Oklahoma City. I very much believe that if you give it a try, your sales will not only increase, but the many hours you save, plus the dollars saved on gasoline driving back and forth across town will be of much value to you.

WHY THE FEDERAL RESERVE CONTROLS THE INTEREST RATES AND HOW YOU MAY PROFIT

In the last few years, I have seen mortgage money available for home loans; then a few months later, the source of money seems to have dried up. When this happens, home construction slows down, credit requirements become strict, and real estate salesmen find they aren't making as many sales and our income has dropped.

Why and how does this happen?

You don't want to blame your loan officer or the

lending institution. The answer is tied to shifts in the *interest rate* and monetary policy of the Federal Reserve system.

You and I can use the information I learned as a banker about the Federal Reserve system in your real estate business. The Federal Reserve Act was passed by Congress and signed by President Wilson in 1913. This act divided the nation into twelve Federal Reserve districts, with a Federal Reserve bank in each district.

The initial capital was obtained by stock subscriptions of commercial banks within a district. The subscribers were known as member banks. The Federal Reserve works hand in hand with the President and the Treasury Department. They are so close that the Federal Reserve could be called the "Central Banking Authority." The basic function of this Authority, the Federal Reserve, is to *influence the interest rate.*

To *make money scarce,* the Federal Reserve *raises* the interest rate to slow the flow of money. The higher the interest rate, the less the supply of money.

To *make money plentiful,* the Federal Reserve *lowers* the interest rate, which increases the flow of money.

You should make it a point to periodically find out the current interest rate the Federal Reserve Bank charges its member banks. You can chart the rise and fall, and use it as a personal barometer. It is simple to find out — just call your banker and ask him. He will tell you. Be sure he understands that you are interested in the rate the Federal Reserve charges him (if this is a member bank, you can tell by the word "National" in the bank name), and not the interest rate he charges *his customers* for personal loans. These consumer rates can vary from customer to customer. It just depends on how loudly he complains when he obtains a loan.

You want to look upon interest as rent paid on money. Money is a commodity like other goods. When scarce, the rent is high; when plentiful, the rent is low. The Federal Reserve controls the money, so it controls the rent. The primary reason for controlling the interest rate is that the Federal Reserve thinks it has a direct effect on inflation or deflation.

Inflation occurs when the spigot is turned on to increase the flow of money. When this happens, there is too much money chasing too few goods.

Deflation is when the supply of goods is more than the supply of money; then the price of goods and services go down.

Here is how the Federal Reserve affects you and I as we deal in real estate. If the Federal Reserve raises the interest rate, home building slows down, mortgage money is hard to find, and the lenders tighten their credit standards. When the rate is lower, housing booms, money is plentiful, and many lenders will even *take* some *marginal* home loans because they have slackened their credit standards.

If you keep a close barometer on the Federal interest rate, you can see the booms and slow downs in advance and adjust your business to meet the rise and fall in the real estate business.

HOW MILLION DOLLAR PRODUCERS OBTAIN LISTINGS ON EXISTING HOMES

When I first entered the real estate field after twenty-five years in lending and banking, I must admit that I often wondered where I was going to get property to sell. The first year was spent with a builder-broker and I sold mostly new homes. But, the day finally comes when you must have existing homes to sell to keep up a sales volume and meet the needs of all prospects.

Have you ever wondered where the real estate salesman who is a million dollar producer and is always at the top in his company, finds listings on existing homes?

Here is his secret:

You know what revenue tax stamps are. They are attached to all mortgages or deeds filed at the County Court House, which makes a public record of the price a buyer pays for his property.

There are many people trying to sell real estate, but actually, there isn't much competition because many sales people sit around in an office or coffee shop waiting for a customer to come around and give them listings. This is one reason for the great mortality rate among real estate people. I have watched many men and women play chauffeur to a new couple in town, just hoping for a sale. Or, they spend hours touring a couple through open houses, when in truth, the prospects just didn't have the money for the movies, so decided to look at new houses instead.

Believe me, after you have learned to qualify a prospect for a home loan and put to use the information this chapter reveals, you will sell more real estate in one year than many other salesmen will sell in ten years.

"How to get listings" on existing homes. First, pick out a street where you think there might be homeowners who would be interested in selling their houses. A good street would be one where you may have seen a sign reading "For Sale By Owner".

Take your notebook and head for the Court House and begin checking the revenue stamps for the last transaction on the street you have selected. You get the names of each homeowner, and by checking the revenue stamps, you find out *what they paid* for their homes. This is permissable and legal, inasmuch as it is all public information. And who is the public? It is you and me.

Now, go back to the neighborhood with all this information. You now have not only the name and address and amount paid for one property, but for the whole street. Next, get out of your car and start walking along the street, making notes on each house — such as the color, type of fence, flowers, and other information that is outstanding about the property. Then go back to the office if you must, but I always go home. For some strange reason, all the sit-arounders in an office always want to know what you are doing. Let them dig their own holes.

The telephone is your next step. You call the man who had the "For Sale By Owner" sign on his lawn. You need to find out how much he wants for his home, for this will serve as a guide for comparable houses we have on our list. Let us say the price is $30,000. You check your list for the homeowner next door, because you are going to start calling each one listed on this street.

Before you call Mr. John Doe on your list, we first want to check on what he paid for his home, which is the information we got from the court house. If Mr. John Doe paid $25,000 for his house, we readily see by our guide of $30,000 that Mr. Doe has a profit of $5,000. You also want to figure the profit on each house you have on your list before making a telephone call. *Profit* is going to be the *key* to our telephone call to the homeowner. You might make your call something like this:

> "Hello, Mr. John Doe, this is Mr. or Ms. Salesperson. I want to congratulate you on the excellent buy you made on your home. It has grown in value from $25,000 which you paid for it, to $30,000. Also, the new stockade fence has increased its value."

What have you accomplished up to this point? The homeowner is probably dumbfounded — for here is someone who not only knows his name, but knows how much he paid for his house and all about the improvements. His response may be just a "Thank you" or a plain "Uh! Huh!" You continue with your sales talk:

> "Mr. Doe, do you know you can make $5,000 profit on your home today? You might consider selling and moving closer to your job. I can show you how to get this nice profit and not pay a penny of tax on the $5,000." Now, ask him if this doesn't sound like it might be worth a few minutes of his time.

If he says, "Yes", you have a fifty-fifty chance of picking up a listing. If he says, "No", try this:

> "I can understand why you don't want to sell, what with the new stockade fence and the yard work you have done, but do you think Mr. Jones or Mr. Smith (pick out a couple of names from your list of his neighbors) would like to make a nice profit on their homes?"

He is going to tell you one of them would like to sell, if for nothing more than to get you off the phone. Then, he might just happen to know of a neighbor who is thinking about selling his house.

I know you are not going to get a listing on each call, but thanks to the good ole' "law of averages," if there is any business on that street, you are going to get it.

Remember, if Mr. Doe had said "yes", you not only get to sell his house, but you may get to sell him a home in another part of town where you have a listing.

Please remember, when a prospective seller or buyer starts to back out on a deal, forget it! Don't waste time on them. Let the sit-arounders at the office have them. Your time is too valuable. You are in the home-selling business to make money.

When you put to use the information in this chapter, you can't help but make huge commissions. These principles and techniques work. I have tried them time and time again, and have continually made more money than I ever thought possible in the real estate business.

Here is a tip that was given to me. I have never tried it, but it sounds good, and if it works it could mean additional sales for you. The *recent seller* of a home could be a good source of prospects.

Having just sold a home, he is probably qualified for a home loan. Also, it could be that having made a nice profit on the house, he has the down payment. You can tell him that you have a house listed where he can do this again. Everyone likes to make a profit on a house. You can usually get recent sellers' names from the real estate pages of newspapers or, back again to old faithful, the court house, where public records of all recent sales are kept. This could be worth a try.

REVEALED — THE SECRETS OF
WHY A PROSPECT
BUYS A HOME

If we knew what prompted each prospect to start house-hunting, our job of matching a couple to a house suitable for their needs and desires would be a simple task.

You may not know each individual case, but you do know that home buyers fall in two categories: (1) Social, and (2) Personal reasons. If you can determine with a few questions, which of the categories our customer fits, you can adapt our sales talk to apply to the prospect and increase your chances of a sale.

Social Reasons

There are many people who have a deep sense of civic responsibility. They feel that owning a home gives them the opportunity to participate in more community affairs. In short, this type of buyer feels the degree to which he can engage in organized activities, the many offices he can hold, or the committees on which he can serve will be greater if he is a homeowner. You can easily recognize this type of person — he most generally wants a house near his church or school where he can always be available to participate in all activities.

When you learn this, you can start checking your listings to meet his needs.

Personal Reasons

Personal reasons may include pride of ownership or peace of mind, but the basic personal reason for buying a home would be security and savings. Ownership of a home gives this person a feeling of independence and security. He reasons that in later years when his home is paid for, regardless of whether there is inflation or depression, he has the security of a roof over his head. He feels more secure than if he was a renter.

This type of man has a deep satisfaction in providing a home for his wife and children. His philosophy is that his future lies in his children. In a sense, home ownership protects his children and the future of his seed.

A recent survey shows that 32% of the new homeowners buy because they like the security of ownership.

Savings

There is an old saying in banking, "Pay yourself first."

How true this is — but Americans have the tendency to pay others first, and then spend for the many pleasures that our good life has to offer, and at the end of the month, there isn't any money left to pay themselves. So, their savings suffer.

One of my banker friends told me that if the majority of his customers missed a month's pay, their savings would be wiped out on bills. The ownership of a home creates a forced savings. The owner must set aside enough money each month for a house payment, taxes, and insurance. Here we could engage in a good debate, "Home ownership versus Renting." But, you are interested in the prospective home-owner, as you want to make a sale, not a rental. Actually, the person who buys a home, from the savings point of view, believes that if you are going to pay rent, why not pay it to yourself?

Once you have determined the motive for buying, you can help the prospect to buy instead of having to sell him a home. We know that when we *help* the prospect *buy* instead of selling him, we have a satisfied customer. The happy homeowner is going to tell his friends and relatives, which means more prospects for us.

While on the subject of why people buy, I want to share some information I have learned in the banking business.

Today, you have computers that you can use to gather information on loan customers, such as the average income, the average length of employment, average age, and much more data. But, in closing loans over many years as a loan officer, I have seen the *influence a woman* has in buying homes. This is information that a computer cannot pick up. You might like to take notes on this information, or better yet, make this book a part of your sales kit.

1. If a woman feels she has failed as a wife or mother — does she blame herself or her husband? Neither. She blames the house she lives in. She can find a hundred things wrong with the place, and if she complains long enough, what happens? The husband will agree to move to another house.

2. When a couple first gets married and are happily hunting for a house, they usually both agree on the type of housing they need. But, after the anniversaries pass by for a few years, who dominates the decision on which house to buy? You guessed it — the wife.

3. In later years, if the wife reaches a point where she feels her sexual attraction has declined, she may feel her "bargaining power" has been reduced, and there is a possibility her husband might find outside interests which are a threat to her security. Real or imaginary, one way the wife can prove herself safe is to have her husband buy things for her. It can be trinkets or diamonds, so long as he is buying things for her — even a new home if she desires. If she thinks he is unfaithful, is there a better way to keep him home than a large monthly house payment? After all, "Home is where the mortgage is."

Just a little summary on this — regardless of age, the wife can be sixteen or sixty years old. They can be in a low income bracket or pay cash for a house — the fact still remains that the wife usually makes the final decision on which house to buy. She may not express herself in your presence, but you can almost bet on it — she will when they get back home. Strange but true.

Imagination in Sales

I would say that next to enthusiasm, imagination plays a great part in every successful real estate salesman. Here are a few pointers that can help to stimulate the imagination of the prospect.

You can remember the slogan of the Buick Automobile Company, "When better cars are built, Buick will build them." The salesmen selling Buicks use this slogan to fire the imagination on how much better their auto was constructed than his competitors'. We just don't want to say that our house is the best buy in the addition. Be enthusiastic and compare the features of your house to a cheaper house. Build up in the prospect's mind the value he is going to receive when he makes the purchase.

I have noticed, and perhaps you have too, that there has been change in advertising over the years, especially on television. For instance, the advertiser will say that his razor is better than brand "X," naming the razor brand. Even the auto buyers are naming the make of competitors, pointing out certain features that are inferior. I have never used this in any of my sales presentations where I would name a realtor or builder as having inferior houses. I hope real estate advertising never comes to this type of advertising.

Pride of Ownership

Pride falls into the category of "social" reasons for owning a home. Pride of ownership is one of the best selling points you can use. You should always speak to the customer as if he had already purchased the house — use the term, "your home." Stimulate his imagination as to what the house will look like when he moves in. Let him see where he can plant roses; let him visualize what a difference a hedge or fence would make. Inplant the pride of ownership in his mind's eye.

Prestige Among Friends

Here the social reason comes in again. It is true that inwardly, every prospect wants to buy a house just a little better than his friends and neighbors — if for nothing more than to just surprise them when he makes the purchase. "Keeping up with the Joneses" is an age old tool of a salesman to stimulate the imagination of the buyer. It is still modern — still the same as yesterday.

Give the prospect plenty of information about a house he is planning to buy. Tell the truth, even if there is a defect. Often, when a defect is mentioned, the customer can sense a bit of honesty. It is our duty to supply the customer the information he requests. Go a little further and give him information he didn't ask about. Remember, a sale can be lost by saying too little, in the same way as you can talk yourself out of a sale by saying too much.

HOW TO PROFIT —
AFTER YOU MAKE THE SALE

There is great satisfaction in a job well done. This is true of a doctor after a successful operation, a lawyer after winning a case, and the real estate salesman after he closes a sale and a home loan. However, salesmen often overlook their customer after they receive their commission. The doctor doesn't. He continues to make routine calls on his patient; the lawyer still services his client. Real estate salesmen should do the same.

Moving into a new home is often a traumatic experience for a family, involving new surroundings, new friends and new neighbors. Now is the time to establish good will. The successful salesman does not forget his customer. He will make an occasional drive by the buyer's house to see if he can be of any assistance. You can offer suggestions on improvement of the home, advice on the location of the best grocery store, and other small things that are helpful.

The family will recognize the salesman as a professional and will recommend him to their friends and relatives who may be in the market to buy or sell a home. You just never know, when you do just a little more than is required, what benefits you will reap.

THE LARGEST PARCEL OF
REAL ESTATE EVER SOLD

Have you guessed who was the salesman and the buyer in this land transaction? Napoleon Bonaparte, the Emperor of France, made the sale, and President Thomas Jefferson, made the buy. The purchase was made in 1803, and was known as the Louisiana Purchase.

The boundaries of the land involved were the Mississippi on the east and the Rocky Mountains on the west; the southern boundary was the Gulf of Mexico, and the tract extended to the north to Canada. The price Napoleon received for this 1,172,000 acres was $15,000,000. The land was later divided into all or part of fourteen states.

This was certainly a bargain and was also the largest real estate deal, not just in the United States, but in the world, as far as land area is concerned.

The largest sum ever paid for a tract of land was a reported $250,000,000 for 12 acres. This was for Rockefeller Center in New York.

It is doubtful whether you or I will ever make this kind of deal. But realize that you fall somewhere in between, and that it *is* possible to sell millions of dollars of real estate today in a short period of time. You are limited only by yourself. It is a known fact that more fortunes are made in real estate than any other field.

Each year there will be approximately 33 million families who will move from one home to another. Roughly 22 million will move only a short distance from their present location, from one neighborhood to another; a small town to another small town; from the middle of the city to the suburbs.

However, only 13 million will cross a county line into another county, and only half of these moves will be across a state line.

It is true that 20% of Americans change the place they live every year. This leaves us with a couple of facts — less than 4% of Americans live out their life span in one dwelling, and less than 15% live in one county all their lives.

These millions must be helped with their real estate transactions. The professional real estate person who "deals" like a millionaire is the one who will make *big money* — *fast*. So, start buying and selling real estate and get a license if you need one. You will have more fun, enjoy more excitement, and make more money than in anything else you can do.

KEY WORDS MOST FREQUENTLY USED BY LOAN OFFICERS

Appraisal: 1. An estimate of value. 2. The process of preparing such an estimate.

Assessed Value: The valuation placed on property by public authority for purposes of taxation.

Attachment: 1. A legal process by which property is taken into custody. 2. The instrument which issues from such a process.

Broker: A middle man who brings together buyers and sellers of the same security or commodity and executes their orders, charging a commission for the service.

Closing a Mortgage Loan: The consummation of a loan transaction in which all appropriate papers are signed and delivered to the lender, in which the making of the mortgage becomes a completed transaction, and in which the proceeds of the mortgage loan are disbursed by the lender to the borrower or upon the borrower's order.

Closing Charges: The expenses or costs incurred in the sale, pledging, or transfer of property, such as recording fees and title examination fees, which must be provided for and distributed between the parties upon the consummation of the transaction.

Cloud on Title: A defect in the chain of title to real property that prevents the acceptance of that title in the market.

Construction Loan: Funds extended on the security of real estate for the purpose of constructing improvements on the property; usually advanced during the period of construction.

Conventional Mortgage Loan: A mortgage loan made directly to the borrower without government insurance or guaranty.

Credit File: An assembly of facts and opinions which indicate the financial resources of an individual (or an enterprise), his character, and his record of performance, especially toward financial obligations.

Deed: A written document that transfers the title to real property from the seller to the buyer.

Deed Restrictions: Provisions inserted in a deed limiting the use of the property conveyed by the deed.

Deficiency Judgment: A court order authorizing collection from a debtor of any part of a debt that remains unsatisfied after foreclosure and sale of collateral.

First Mortgage: A legal instrument that creates or conveys a lien on or a claim against an owner's rights in property prior to a lien created by any other mortgage.

Foreclosure: The legal process by which a mortgagor of real or personal property, or other owner of property subject to a lien is deprived of his interest therein. The usual modern method is the sale of the property by court proceedings or outside of court.

Guaranty Policy: A contract in which one party, the guarantor, agrees to indemnify or protect another party against loss because of certain specified hazards.

Housing Expenses: The total of all items of expenditure incurred in connection with the occupancy of housing facilities, except expenses attributable to furniture and furnishings or to capital charges.

Instrument: A written document that gives formal expression to a legal act or agreement.

Interest: The sum paid for the use of borrowed money or credit.

Justified Price: The price which an informed and prudent purchaser would be warranted in paying.

Lien: An encumbrance on an owner's title to real property.

Maturity: The due date of a mortgage, note, draft, acceptance, bond or other instrument.

Merchantable Title: That condition of title which is acceptable in the market.

Mortgagee: One who lends money on the security of a mortgage.

Net Worth: The excess of the assets of an individual or an enterprise over all his or its liabilities.

Note (as used in mortgage lending): A written promise, secured by a mortgage, to pay a certain amount or amounts at a specified date or dates or on stipulated conditions.

Open Mortgage Loan: A past-due mortgage loan which is being held by the mortgagee without requiring refinancing or the execution of an extension agreement.

Possession: The right to exclusive occupancy and use of real property.

Prepayment: Any amount paid to reduce the principle of a mortgage loan in advance of the due date or in excess of the stipulated amortization.

Real Estate Owned: A term that applies to all real estate directly owned by a bank, usually not including real estate taken to satisfy a debt.

Recourse: The right to require performance of an obligation by an endorser, assignor, or other prior holder of an instrument.

Refinancing: The payment of indebtedness with funds obtained through the creation of a new obligation or obligations.

Reserve (as used in mortgage lending): Funds set aside for a particular purpose, usually to protect the security of outstanding mortgage loans.

Risk Analysis: An examination of the elements or sources of risk in a mortgage loan and of their effects both separately and in combination.

Risk Rating: A systematic process of analyzing mortgage risk that results in estimation, in precise relative terms, of the soundness of individual transactions.

Term (of a mortgage loan): The period of time extending from the original date of a mortgage loan to the date of its maturity.

Unencumbered Property: Property that is free and clear of assessments, liens, easements and exceptions of all kinds.

Waiver: The voluntary relinquishment of a right, privilege or advantage. The instrument evidencing such an act frequently is known as a waiver.

Zoning: The process of establishing, by legislation, certain restrictions upon the use to which property may be put.

CHAPTER TEN

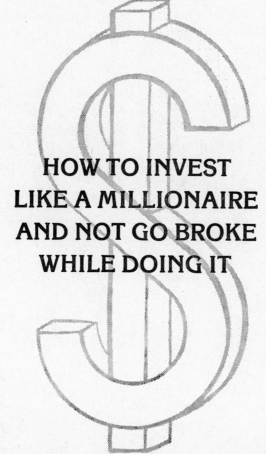

HOW TO INVEST
LIKE A MILLIONAIRE
AND NOT GO BROKE
WHILE DOING IT

BUY — BUY — BUY. You are bombarded daily by television, radio, newsprint and the man on the street, to buy something. Often, you are caught up in the frenzy and come home with a potato peeler that doesn't work, or even worse, a hand full of worthless stock certificates.

It is a strange fact of life that 99% of the bad deals you make are due to the fact that you know nothing about the product or the investment deal you put your money in. If everyone invested only in what they had some knowledge of, half the losses in the world would stop.

The amateur investor always wants to make a killing — he is never satisfied with a 10% profit. He wants to double his money quickly. This same cautious businessman knows he can't make these kinds of profits in his own business, but he will invest his money in some promotion thousands of miles from home.

I have seen businessmen chase rainbows in the money world. I have seen men who are most practical about their banking affairs invest several thousand dollars in worthless stock promotions — some in deals as far away as Africa.

The old saying that "life begins at 40" may be true, but I would say your investment life begins at 40. Almost every man at 40 years of age has tucked away somewhere a little bundle of worthless paper — with beautiful printed words on the face, "Stock Certificate." About all they are worth is the cost of the ink to print them.

We know one man in Dallas, Texas, who refers to his worthless stock certificate as his "Diploma in Finance." In other words — it was his education. However, he could have attended the best university in Texas for the price he paid for the worthless stock. He bought through ignorance, or a lack of knowledge. If he had known anything about the business deal, he would still have his money.

The price is too great for an education when you can just as easily learn from the simple statement "buy only what you have some knowledge of." If you don't know, get expert advice from your banker or tax accountant. They would be disinterested parties and could probably save you thousands of dollars in some worthless promotion.

Having worked twenty-five years in the banking and lending industry, I must let you know that at the top of the pyramid in the financial world there are many trustworthy bankers and money managers who watch over our monetary system. But, at the bottom of the pyramid, in this jungle of finance, are some of the most unscrupulous con artists and swindlers that you can imagine, and the majority work just inside the law. Many are church members and pillars in their communities — but when it comes to promoting a scheme on the unsuspecting, they close their eyes to all morals and fleece more money from the public than all the armed robbers combined in the United States.

Curiously, the restaurant down the street could sell you a bad steak and could wind up being sued or pay a heavy fine, but a broker or a money manager can sell liabilities and debts as assets and cash, and everyone thinks he is a shrewd businessman.

When you begin to "deal" in the world of investing, the first lesson to learn is to "doubt everything you hear," because you will be flooded with hot tips. But please remember, a tip is only an opinion — and opinions are like noses, everybody has one.

In addition, nine times out of ten, if you receive a tip to buy, it's coming from the seller, and if it's a tip to sell, it comes from the buyer. If you doubt this, walk into any broker's office and ask him — very few will deny it.

In the world of finance, everyone is concerned about something, and will stretch the truth out of proportion to promote their own scheme to part someone from his money.

One group is rushing around trying to push up prices; others are trying to push prices down — and somewhere the truth gets lost in the shuffle.

Recently a customer brought me a prospectus — and believe me, the flowery words and projected profits would almost persuade anyone to buy shares in a franchise selling ice cream on the moon. Remem-

ber, a prospectus is like a tip. There are some copy-
writers who can write a prospectus on a garbage
truck and make it look like a Cadillac.

Don't overlook advertisements. Some are about
as true as Snow White and the Seven Dwarfs. Most
magazines and newspapers will print anything with
no questions asked. However, regarding stock offers,
the SEC has guidelines on advertising, but you still
are invited to send for a prospectus which shows
balance sheets and projected growth and profits.

Have your CPA look over balance sheets — often
losses are shown as gains, and some have enough
water to float a battleship.

One strange thing about human nature — someone tells an untruth and few people will believe it.
But, write it in an advertisement or print in a newspaper, and half the people will believe it as gospel
truth. Simply because they read it.

Never, never buy unless you have some knowledge of the business. For example, if you own a clothing store, buy stock in the company that sells you the
best suits. You have knowledge that the company is
stable and making a profit.

If you are a bus driver, invest in the bus company that has the best management and has a record
of dependability.

If you are a real estate salesman, buy houses or
apartments — something you have some knowledge
of.

If you are a doctor or nurse, buy shares in an
old reliable pharmaceutical manufacturer.

But that's not all. Don't overlook the small factory or plant in your own town. You live there and can
watch the progress in your own community.

The grass always looks greener on the other
side of the fence, but if you had to pay for the mowing
with your own savings, it might not look so good.

Always invest in a business that you have some

knowledge of. You may be an amateur in investing, but you don't have to lose your money through ignorance. It's hard to fool a man in a business he knows.

Ignorance in investing is dangerous — it borders on gambling. In fact, investing in ignorance is more risky than betting on a horse race. No one knows for sure which horse to bet on unless the race is fixed. When you invest without some knowledge of the business you are putting your money in, the same odds are against your winning as a horse race, and you never know if the investment deal is fixed.

I know this is true, because there is more money invested in gold mines than there is gold taken out.

Here is one common fact of life — just ask any person who is wealthy — very few people will tell you the truth. There are honest and dishonest people who will try everything to transfer money from your pocket to theirs.

Be cautious. When approached to buy or invest, ask yourself, "Do I know anything about it?" If not, let someone else have the deal, or hire an expert. You will be thousands of dollars richer.

HOW TO INVEST IN STOCKS
THAT WILL GUARANTEE YOU
A FAST FORTUNE

Everyone has a system — the butcher, the baker, and the candle stick maker. All have game plans on how to make a profit from their business. That is the way it should be, but when most of us think of a system, our thoughts turn to some type of system to beat the odds in gambling.

Every gambler has his pet system, from simple chicken tracks on a piece of paper to elaborate computer print-outs. If you don't have a system to beat the odds at the dice tables or horse races, you can buy one.

But, please remember, many a person has gone to a gambling resort in a $15,000 automobile, with a "perfect system," only to return home on a $100,000 Greyhound Bus (if they had enough money left to buy a ticket.)

The information we are going to share with you on how to invest in stocks is a *system* — not advice. It works for me. If it doesn't work for you, then you must find your own system.

First — It takes nerve. But, as I mentioned in the first chapter, to "deal like a millionaire" you must take the attitude of nothing ventured, nothing gained.

Second — It takes a little research. You must locate an industry that is in a slump. It could be the TV industry, oil, steel, mining, peanuts or any major industry. Notice we said industry, not company.

Third — you must find the best company in that industry which has plenty of cash reserves and limited debts. Usually this company has been in business for several years.

Here is what happens. When the industry hits the slide downward, the company you selected is pulled down with all the rest. What should we do?

Fourth — You should buy shares in the company you have selected. But you must purchase common shares (See glossary, Chapter 8), because they go down the quickest and farthest.

Now, what have we accomplished? You have purchased stock in the best company in a depressed industry. You are betting (that's why we call it a system) on an industry — not a company. The odds are in your favor — no industry remains in a slump forever.

If you are over thirty years old you have seen all the industries in the U.S.A. have their ups and downs.

Now you have a simple system that can make you a fast fortune. The information is for the select few who have the nerve and the money to play the stock market.

Remember, you can buy fancy worded newsletters, and you can buy gold bordered brochures that explain the hows, whens and wheres of the stock market — just as you can buy systems to beat the horses — but knowledge alone won't make you a winner. It takes wisdom, which is applied knowledge. It means you must be motivated to action.

If a hunter gave you his secret on how to kill a grizzly bear, very few people would rush to the forest to get one. The same is true of our secret, yet simple system on how to invest in the stock market. As I mentioned, the system is mine — if it doesn't work for you, hunt your own grizzly.

As a banker, I could tell you to keep your money in a savings account and be satisfied with a 5-1/2% or 7% interest, whatever the going rate — but I am writing this book for the few people who wish to "deal" like millionaires and get rich on borrowed money.

We have learned in the financial world that money is often created out of thin air — and there is more than enough for every one. So, it is my purpose to show you how to make as much money as you wish and, at the same time, hold your own against anyone who tries to take it away.

As I previously mentioned, I don't give advice on securities or legal matters. Always get professional advice. However, keep in mind that if you want to keep your money safe, always buy government bonds. If the government folds it won't make any difference where your money is anyway — but that's unlikely.

If you like to speculate, buy preferred stocks. But, if you are really just looking for excitement buy common stocks. Then you can read market quotations daily, just like a racing form. The odds for winning are just about the same.

At this point, let me say the stock market exchanges are the backbone of our capitalist system. The stock market is just as valuable to our free enterprise system as the airlines and the railroads. Those who don't understand how and why it works cry out that it is a place where only fools will tread — that it is a den of robbers — "stay away" they howl. Those who use this line of reason would also tell us to stay away from Interstate 40 because five people were killed there last week.

It is true that a lot of people have lost their shirts in the stock market, but remember this one fact — where there is a loser, there must be a winner. The stock market is not for the faint hearted or the uninformed.

One point to keep in mind — stock prices do not reflect the true value of a stock. They represent the emotions of men. It tells you the signs of the times. The exchange is a barometer of the current market conditions. Almost anything can affect the rise and fall of stock prices — the weather, presidential elections, war news, a major strike, Federal Reserve control of interest rates, even a wheat crop.

If you are going to invest in stocks, you must learn to turn a deaf ear to public opinions and learn how to determine the true value of a security.

To further help you invest in stock, I would like for you to add the following suggestion to your simple system, then make a test for a few weeks before you invest any money. Keep accurate records of your paper profits and losses. If it works for you, you are on your road to a fast fortune.

1. *Pick out five different stocks.*
2. *Pick those that you have some knowledge of.*

3. Pick stocks of companies that are at least three years old.

4. Pick as many as possible that have branches or plants in your own city.

5. Pick only stocks that are traded on the big board.

6. Pick stock from at least five different industries.

To begin your test, watch the industry you picked that began to slide. When this begins, the stock you selected in that industry will also begin to go down in price. When it reaches a low for the year — that is the time to purchase. Figure a 25% profit and this would be your selling price. When the industry begins its upswing, the price of the company stock you picked will start to rise.

When it reaches your pre-determined 25% selling price — SELL! Don't wait to see if it will go higher. As I mentioned in the first chapter, small profits add up. Time is not on your side to build a fortune — *Quick profits are the only answer.*

THE SECRET OF BUYING
WHEN EVERYONE IS SELLING
— AND SELLING WHEN
EVERYONE IS BUYING

The day you learn the secret of buying from a pessimist and sell to the optimist, you will be able to build a fortune even the super-rich would envy. However, few people have the courage to break away from the crowd and "deal" like a millionaire.

Most people follow the crowd hysteria — when the crowd sells, they sell — when the crowd buys, they buy. Even some of the most experienced investors forget to think for themselves and join in the march along with the crowd.

To learn how the crowd reacts to news events, make a trip to one of the large brokerage houses, and just listen to the talk of the day — 99% is just plain gossip. And, at the large exchanges, you will always find a crowd. You will see the crowd that is buying and the crowd that is selling. Most beginners, when they enter the investment world, always join the biggest crowd — and usually it is the crowd of losers.

It seems that by human nature we tend to follow the biggest crowd, just like cattle, we tend to drift if we don't have someone to guide us.

Why do we follow? Because often we don't want to seem out of place or unfriendly, and it could be just because it is easier and we don't have to think. We allow various groups to tell us what to do. Even our neighbors tend to form our opinion. Last but not least — television. We are told what to eat and what to wear, until conformity seems the popular thing to do.

If you are going to "deal" like a millionaire, you must break away from the crowd and not conform your life to the life of the masses or crowds. There may be safety in numbers, but certainly not in investing, because the crowd always loses. This is a secret of money managers and they are not going to broadcast it to the public.

In investing there are few winners, but they do it by determing values — not by following the crowd. Investing is different than politics. Money doesn't care who gets how many votes.

There are various factors that affect prices in the money market — the greatest is public opinion, which has no bearing on the value of a security.

In addition, when fifty people want to sell the same thing and only ten people want to buy — what happens? The price goes down. If ten people are selling and you have fifty buyers — the price goes up.

As you develop the ability to "deal" you will

learn to stand back from the crowd and watch the price go up and down. Then you buy at the bottom and sell at the top.

As I mentioned, if you follow the largest crowd in politics you win — but not in money matters. You join the smallest group or better yet, stand alone, if you really want to learn the art of "dealing" like a millionaire and getting rich on borrowed money.

Please remember this one fact in our economic system, prices are never constant. They are always moving up or down. This tells us one thing — never buy when there are too many buyers, because you will pay too much. Never sell when there are more sellers than buyers — you will get too little for your goods.

If you would like to see this principal in action, attend an auction. The prices are governed by the number of buyers or the number of sellers. With a little nerve and experience you can become a master at buying at the bottom and selling at the top, and accumulate a fortune you never dreamed possible.

The question comes to my mind as to why does the crowd buy when the prices are high and sell when prices are low? It is simple to answer — they have never learned to "think money." They never look any further than one day ahead. They think the present conditions will last forever.

If the country is in a recession, they think it will never end, and you have the crowd of pessimists. Let a boom arrive, and this same crowd becomes optimists.

But, the man who gets rich — *(please read carefully)* is opposite the crowd — *he becomes an optimist (a buyer) during a recession and a pessimist (a seller) during a boom.*

If you can grasp this principal, you are on your road to becoming a millionaire. It is the man who understands this money-making principal and keeps a level head when the crowd stampedes like cattle, who becomes a leader.

People are influenced by their hopes and fears — prices always go up and down — but seldom do they go out of sight in either direction. That is why you can buy when everyone is selling and sell when everyone is buying — and become a millionaire during the process.

HOW TO SELECT WHAT TO BUY THAT CAN BE SOLD AT HUGE PROFITS

How many times have you purchased a "white elephant" — bought something you couldn't give away, much less sell and get your money back.

You couldn't do this many times or you would go broke. Never buy anything that you can't resell for a profit.

I have seen some good businessmen go out of business and many people lose their savings, because they didn't follow this simple rule.

Never buy something just because it pleases your fancy — of course if you have plenty of money to indulge in this luxury — fine.

Almost every new businessman makes this mistake. If he is in the clothing business, he buys clothes he likes and finds no one likes his taste — and he has his shelves full of clothes that are a loss.

In the past ten years, while in the real estate business, I have seen dozens of people make mistakes in building houses. I have seen couples build a house in an out of the way place, and call it their "dream home." Several years later, they wish to sell, and no one will buy. It is too far from anywhere, or too exotic in design. No one wants another man's folly.

We know one man who built an underground home, and spent over $50,000 to complete it. Today he can't sell it for $10,000. All he has is a well-furnished storm cellar — which may be a fine place to be during tornado season here in Oklahoma — but, it certainly isn't worth a $40,000 loss just to please oneself.

Remember the story of the man who bought 100 shares of stock at $1.00 and each day he called his broker to get the price quote. Each day the broker would tell him they had increased $10.00 per share. When they reached $100.00 per share, the buyer gave the order to sell. The broker gave the classic answer, "Sell to whom?"

He wants to sell, but nobody wants to buy. Almost every man has bought something he can't sell, but we don't have to make it a habit.

Here are some facts to keep in mind before making any major purchase:

1. *Prices are made by supply and demand, not by true value. Price is simply what someone will pay for it.*

2. *You may change your mind — the thing you like today may displease you tomorrow.*

3. *Don't spend money to satisfy ego and think you made an investment.*

4. *The more exotic or unique a product or property, the less the number of buyers.*

The mass of people want things that are mass-produced. This is a secret almost all advertisers know, and they sell tons of merchandise.

Always look at anything you purchase as money — money can always be excahnged for products or services. If you invest in the stock market, you know that shares in IBM can be sold by picking up the telephone and calling any broker. But, shares in some little known computer company may be a "white elephant." You can't find anyone to buy them at any price.

The secret to the value of anything is "Can it be resold at a profit?" In addition, there is no market for anything that people have never heard of.

Our Capitalist system is geared to a simple process — money changing into goods and services — and goods and services into money. With a profit, of course, on each exchange.

If we don't make a profit, we either go broke or wind up with a charitable organization. So, that is why, when you make a major purchase, ask yourself the question "Will someone else buy it at a higher price?" If the answer is yes, buy. It is the nearest thing to a sure profit as anything in our Capitalist system.

As we mentioned, if you want to see this principal in operation, attend an auction. The auctioneer puts up a lamp for sale — everybody can use a lamp. Ten people bid and run the price to $75.00. The actual value of the lamp could be $50.00. Then you see a piece of glassware go on the auction block — three people bid and it sells for $10.00. The true value could be $150.

It's this one principal you must remember as you "deal" like a millionaire — unless you have money to burn — buy only what you can resell at a profit. And remember, value is based on the saleability, a fact never to be overlooked.

HOW TO BE ON GUARD
FROM THOSE WHO WISH TO
SEPARATE YOU FROM
YOUR MONEY

When you have accumulated money, you should make it a rule — never invest or lend money on the spur of the moment. There are so many friends, relatives and outright beggers, that you must always be on guard.

You must learn to say "no" to the silver-tongued parasites who feed themselves by talking other people out of their money.

Always, when you are approached for money — never make a decision until you have slept on it. You may save yourself several thousand dollars. This world is filled with people who have developed the fine art of talking people out of their money. Often, they are so persuasive they are hard to resist. You must build up a resistance to them, just like building up your body to resist disease.

In the world of money making, there are people who can separate you from your money and never use a gun. Some try for ten dollars, others for ten million — but they call it transfer money, from your pocket to theirs. None do an honest day's work. They are constantly painting beautiful pictures of some wonderful scheme to make millions. They cry, "Hurry! Hurry! Your last chance." This always draws a crowd, it can be at a broker's office or at a carnival — their purpose is the same — to separate you from your money, and it isn't long until the con man has the money and the people have "the beautiful scheme."

There is no law against a person being fooled. But you can protect yourself if you adopt the attitude that you *"will never invest under crowd hysteria or high pressure."*

But it isn't always the stranger that applies the pressure to get your money from your pocket to theirs. It can be your closest friend or relative. They set themselves up with all types of reasons that you should give, share or lend them money. You must learn to build up a resistance.

Self-interest isn't selfishness — it is a virtue. It is what keeps our investments on an even keel. It is the thief and begger who invented the thought that self-interest was wrong and that all should share and share alike.

You have earned your money — and you should exercise your right to keep it. This is just plain common sense.

One of the Ten Commandments says you shall not steal. It could have gone a little further and said, "you shall not be stolen from."

One of the least used secrets of keeping your money is overlooked by men who have become wealthy — *talk it over with your wife* before making any major decision with your money. It is a fact that women are more suspicious about investing and lending than men. It is by nature that they would rather have a bird in hand than two in the bush.

A man might make money faster, but it is the woman who can keep it. The man loves the excitement of a "deal," the woman loves the prize.

For example, notice any couple at the state fair — the man may be intent on knocking over the milk bottles with a fast ball, but the lady looks only at the teddy bear or the prize. This is also true in the money world. Get advice from your wife or mother before any major investment deal.

Please remember this point — there is no reason on earth that you should hand over your money to another person, simply because he has a persuasive personality or you can't answer his questions. Never give anyone your money unless you get a fair value in return.

When a person approaches you with a scheme and no money and wants to share a fortune making a gadget or an offer to buy the city park, and insists that you must do it right now, just inform your man that he can have it all for himself. After all, he saw it first.

Dean Wright, an entrepreneur friend of mine from El Paso, has two slogans on his desk. One sign says, "Do it now" — the other reads, "What I have — I Keep".

You might place them on your desk, and when a

man with a wild idea and no money in his wallet
comes, just simply point to the sign on your desk. If
he says the deal is now or never, simply say "never."
Many a man has saved his hard earned money by
adopting this method of protecting his money.

It may be true. There may be times when it is a
valid deal and there is an opportunity to make a large
sum of money by quick action, but if you don't have
time to check it out, pass it by.

You are "dealing" like a millionaire when you are
playing your own game, and always go slow when
you are about to part with your money.

You can lose in 15 minutes what you have earned
in a year.

In addition, you must be on guard against not
only individuals who would like to separate you from
your money, but organizations, namely shady charitable organizations. You know the dozens of requests
for charity contributions that come to your attention.
If you gave to all you would soon be asking for charity
yourself. However, there are worthy ones. But, how
can we be on guard? Here are a few tips:

Door to Door — You should get the solicitors name
and the name of the charity he represents. If he
is selling goodies, such as candy and such, ask
how much goes to his charity. Also, find out
where you can learn more about his group. Always pay by check and make it payable to a
charity, not an individual.

Telephone Solicitation — You should use the same
care as if the caller was in your store or home.
Get name and address of caller, and the name of
charity. Then have him submit his request in
writing. If the caller refuses, you will probably
save yourself some money for a worthy cause
later.

Mail Solicitation — Keep a watchful eye on any
solicitation that comes in the form of a bill or

statement. If items are enclosed that you haven't ordered, the letter should state that you are under no obligation to pay for them or return them. The letter should give the name and address of the charity and where to get additional information. Always pay by check. Never — never — never send cash, even for small amounts.

Here is advice you should follow. When in doubt, check with your local Better Business Bureau. It could save you hundreds of dollars. We all want to give, but give wisely.

MONEYWISE INVESTMENT GUIDELINES THAT COULD MAKE YOU A FORTUNE ALMOST OVERNIGHT

The inside secret of millionaires is simple enough, *"Why Work for Money — When You Can Make Money Work for You!!"*

Of course, you need a few dollars to start with. When you have saved a few dollars, there are ways to make your money multiply for you. Your own banker will tell you that you need a good investment program, and the smart thing to do would be to start investing right now.

Okay, you only have a few dollars to spare. Start by putting them in a savings account. Once your savings account tops out at $1,000, it is time to hunt for a better return on your money. With the inflation rate increasing yearly, money holed up in a savings account loses more in purchasing power than it earns in interest each year. Your same dollar could possibly grow at a greater rate if it was invested in a program elsewhere.

Investments not only keep you ahead of inflation, but they can offer you certain tax savings.

Remember, there are no great secrets to investing your money wisely, but there are *Moneywise Guidelines* that a person can follow on his road to dealing like a millionaire.

Investment Guideline #1

Invest Surplus Money Only. Make it a cardinal rule never to invest money that puts groceries on the table or from an emergency fund you have saved for a rainy day.

It is true that there are certain types of investments that are just as safe as your insured savings account, but you must be prepared to leave your money alone. Many times, if you are forced to withdraw from an investment program, you stand to lose a considerable amount of your money.

Investment Guideline #2

Investigate Before You Invest. This is a slogan of bankers and you should make it your own.

This applies to land, stocks, bonds, or any other investment opportunity that is presented to you. I agree, you can't be an expert in everything, but you should know a little about the game you are putting your money in. You should put in as much time on learning about your investment as you do when buying a house or a new automobile.

Investment Guideline #3

Decisions Based on Emotions. When you put your money in an investment, it is figures on paper that make profits, not our like or dislike for a company or its products.

It isn't always a popular product that is the most profitable. However, it is good judgment to buy stock in a company whose products are in demand year after year.

Strange but true, it is easier to keep your emotions out of your decisions when buying than when selling.

Recently, I purchased stock in a company that I liked because they used the "party plan" type of retailing — it was a good buy; the stock went up and up. But, when the price of the stock began to decline in price, I wouldn't sell because I liked their retailing program. Today, my stock is worth about half what I paid for it. *Lesson Learned* — Keep emotions and prejudices out of your investment programs.

Investment Guideline #4

Keep on Top of Your Investment. Many years ago, you could buy a top quality stock, put it up and collect your interest and dividend checks year after year. Not so today, there are too many changes because things move too fast. Study your investments regularly. If they are not up to your expectations, make a change. Keep a constant check on the market price of your stocks and bonds.

Investment Guideline #5

Advice from Brokers. It is unwise to put too much faith in the advice of a broker. True, they often have knowledge to pass on to their clients, but they are human and make mistakes. Then, he could be asked to push certain stocks the brokerage house is trying to unload. Remember, a broker works on commission — he makes money on every purchase or sale he makes — even if you lose your shirt in the transaction. It is hard for them not to recommend frequent trades in stocks, especially if he has a car payment due or needs money. They are in business to make money for themselves, and they have a standard of living to maintain. Don't rely too much on their suggestions — *do some of the homework yourself.*

Investment Guideline #6

Buy Listed Stocks. The stock market is the most popular type of investment, at least it is the most widely known. Remember, stock prices are determined by the law of supply and demand. There are many factors that determine this that have nothing to do with the profits of the company. Many times, when a company is showing a good profit, the price of its stock goes down. The stock market is a risky investment, but you can reduce the risk if you stay with listed stocks because they have met certain requirements before they are listed on the exchange and tend to be less risky than unlisted stocks traded on what is known as "over the counter" trades. There are exceptions to the rule, for you will find many good bank stocks that are unlisted. But, by far, the risk is less when you buy listed stocks only. Try to stay with well-established companies.

Investment Guideline #7

Stocks That Pay Regular Dividends. The corporations that have paid dividends year after year are the safest, but the company that pays the highest isn't always the best. It is hard to make an unwise decision on a corporation that pays a good healthy dividend regularly.

Investment Guideline #8

Diversify Your Stocks. Never put all your cookies in the same jar. If you have all your money in one company or one type of industry, your chance of a big loss is greater if there is a reversal in that industry or company. It is best to spread your money around. If you don't have that much money, maybe you should take a look at Mutual Funds.

Investment Guidelines #9

Stop Your Losses. The hardest thing for a beginner is to sell his stock at a loss. When you hesitate to sell, it often results in a bigger loss as the price of a stock continues to drop. Here is a good rule to follow when your stock drops below 10% of what you paid. Start thinking seriously about selling. You can

always buy it back if it starts to climb again. If it
doesn't come back, you can use the loss as a tax deduction and invest your money elsewhere.

Investment Guideline #10

Lock Certificates in Safe Deposit Box. When you
purchase a stock, have it registered in your name
and sent to you. It is easier to let the broker keep
them for you, but they do go broke and it could be
months before you could get your certificate, even if
they are insured. You might suffer a loss if you
wanted to sell and you couldn't get your hands on
your stock certificate. I keep mine in a bank safety
deposit box. Never leave them around the house
where fire might destroy them or a thief might steal
them.

Investment Guideline #11

Research Your Stock. You must judge each stock
on its own merit. You must get all the material possible and check company records. Your broker can
help obtain these for you. You can obtain *FREE
BOOKLETS* on investing from the New York Stock
Exchange, 11 Wall Street, New York, New York,
10005.

Investment Guideline #12

Cost of Commissions. The small investor seldom worries about cost of trading, because he is concerned about picking the right stock. But, you should
keep tabs on costs, because they are moving upward
— especially if you are trading 200 shares or less.

Stock exchanges limit trading to members, which
means you do your buying and selling through a
registered representative of the exchange — a broker.
Fees will vary according to the price and number of
shares you trade.

There are ways to reduce costs. For example,
some corporations allow stockholders to use their

dividends to buy additional stocks. In fact, A.T.&T. gives a 5% discount off the market price on such a plan. Maybe the company you have stock with will do the same thing.

Another way to help reduce commission cost is to use discounters, who are located mostly in large cities. However, some will accept phone or mail orders for trades. To get information on this, write: Stockcross, 141 Milk Street, Boston, Mass. 02109.

We would suggest you also check on bank investment plans if your bank participates in those types of service for its customers.

Investment Guideline #13

Bond Markets. A bond is an instrument issued by the government or a company in exchange for a loan. They are as good as the ability of the company to pay. So, consider the rating of the one issuing the bonds. The ratings range from AAA to D — any broker or banker who sells bonds can get you this information.

Good bonds are less risky than stocks and usually pay a higher interest rate than savings accounts. Many people who are looking for a regular income from their investments buy bonds. Let's look at different types of bonds:

1. *Federal Bonds are as good as the government — if the government folds, it won't make much difference anyway — but that isn't likely to happen in our lifetime.*

2. *Municipal Bonds may be your answer if you are in a high income tax bracket. The interest is free from taxes by the Federal and most state governments. These bonds are issued by state and local governments to raise money for roads, schools, etc. However, the rates are usually lower than Corporate or Federal Bonds.*

3. *Corporate Bonds, as a rule, pay the highest rates. However, there is one drawback — they often*

have a clause that allows them to pay off the bonds if interest rates drop. One little secret to use is to try to get the high rate guaranteed for the life of the bond.

Investment Guideline #14

Mutual Funds. If you are a small investor or just don't wish to research or keep on top of your investments, you should consider a mutual fund. A mutual fund, in layman's language, is a company that pools the money of many investors to buy different securities.

You get a couple of advantages. First, all your money doesn't go into one stock — it is spread around several different corporations.

Second, you have pros to manage your money — their fees are paid out of the earnings of the company which usually run less than 1%.

Keep this in mind — some funds make fortunes for their investors and others lose money. Select your mutual fund company just as carefully as any other investment you make.

Check with your banker. He should be able to help you get any information you need on Mutual Funds.

Investment Guideline #15

Other Investment Opportunities. Remember, stocks, bonds and mutual funds are not the only investment opportunity — I know people who deal in commodities, but they are experts. I know people who "deal" like millionaires in antiques, coins, art treasures, and many other things.

It is a fact of life that there are rich and broke people in all business and investment programs, but the greatest majority are *making big money fast.*

Your success in making money could come faster than you think, depending upon how fast you make your start.

CHAPTER ELEVEN

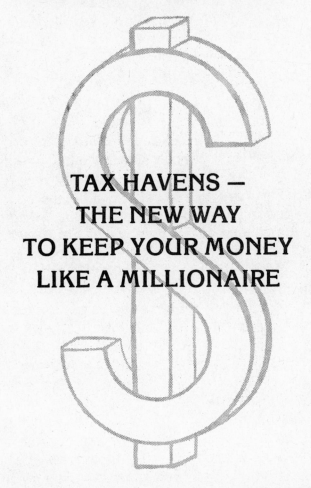

TAX HAVENS —
THE NEW WAY
TO KEEP YOUR MONEY
LIKE A MILLIONAIRE

The purpose of this chapter is to let you know that tax havens do exist, and you can start thinking of them in terms of legal tax avoidance to protect your money.

Many millionaires and other Americans take advantage of the tax savings in havens of foreign countries. It is not our intent to encourage you to use this information as a substitute for your tax accountant or attorney. Always, when "dealing" like a millionaire, get current professional legal and tax advice.

HOW BANKING RULES IN FOREIGN COUNTRIES FAVOR YOU, THE AMERICAN TAX-PAYER — YOUR MONEY IS OFTEN SAFER THERE

Before you can begin to understand tax havens, you must understand certain reasons for their existance. In the last few years the protection of money, whether $100 or a million has become increasingly difficult. In order to stave depreciation, people have resorted to many types of hopeful schemes.

To the follower of money survival, the so-called tax havens that have proven money traps are well known. Many have been stocks, scotch whiskey futures, land deals, silver speculation. We can think of dozens.

The purpose of this chapter is to show you certain tax havens that are considered the most safe in today's unsafe world of economic fluctuation.

First you must understand the difference between tax avoidance and tax evasion. Every country has some system for collecting taxes. In democratic countries, tax laws are passed with a fine line in mind. That line is that the government must collect enough taxes to carry on its functions while at the same time, leaving enough growth money among the people; taxpayers, which naturally includes all people in the country, even those employed by the government. Speculative capital is essential for an economy to keep going to encourage economic growth.

In other words, when a government takes too much money from the people in taxes and then wastes that tax money foolishly, there is not nearly enough venture capital left in the country to maintain a peak gross national product. Of what worth are entrepreneurs when money to put the *new* ideas into being is not available because of a greedy and stifling government?

Such a government eventually falls. Caesar's Rome fell because of a top heavy bureaucracy — not because of too much economic freedom for the people. On the other hand, a corrupt government, too lax in tax collection, is doomed to fall, too. So that is the fine line — collecting enough taxes to run an efficient and prudent government, yet leaving the maximum money in the hands of the people to stimulate economic growth.

Second, tax avoidance is the opposite of tax evasion. The taxpayer who understands every possible deduction and takes advantage of every legal provision of the tax code, is one who practices tax avoidance — *a perfectly legal maneuver.*

In this chapter, you will be shown legal ways to protect your money and see it grow in worldwide tax havens. Whether you pay taxes on your tax haven capital growth depends on current tax laws.

Most countries do not tax their citizens on capital appreciation outside the country. For example, Japanese do not pay individual income tax on money outside Japan until the money is brought back to Japan. Overseas Japanese capital can grow and grow in tax havens without being whittled away by domestic taxes. And when growing in a tax free haven, the Japanese capitalist can spend the money freely outside Japan without paying any taxes to anyone. This is also currently true for Australians and citizens of Great Britain, as well as other countries.

Also, under present laws, Canadians do not pay taxes to their country on money earned abroad when the individual lives abroad. Americans, on the other hand, do have to pay taxes to America when we live and work overseas.

As much as Americans are admired by millions

all over the world, few foreigners realize the individual American is so heavily taxed. With this in mind, the tax haven information in this chapter will give some relief to those Americans who take advantage of what is written here.

Most of the tax havens will have their consulate in the United States. You can write to those which most interest you and you will receive information concerning banks, attorneys and accountants there. You can handle the haven transaction without leaving your home — you do not need to travel abroad.

If you are opening a personal savings account in any haven, it is a simple matter. But, if you want to establish a tax shelter, you will certainly want to retain an attorney or accountant in that country.

Since this is an introduction to tax havens, it should not be considered as a substitute for either legal or tax advice. It would be prudent to see your own attorney and accountant before making your final decision.

With our tax laws due for an overhaul, you will want to get up-to-the-minute information before acting.

You know we live in a fast world — tax havens change too. Governments pass new laws that limit or restrict tax haven advantages. So, it is doubly important to get current information from the consulate, embassy or haven bank, as well as the U.S.A. tax position at the time you make your financial moves.

Now, let's look at some of the more favorable tax haven countries.

Canada

While Canada is not often thought of as a tax haven, there are banking rules that favor U.S.A. citizens and their transactions with Canadian banks.

First, you must keep in mind that Canada is the world's second largest country with only a little more than 20 million people, and with plentiful natural resources hardly scratched. With recent international developments, specifically countries with an over-abundance of natural resources attempting to get the top dollar faster than international economic stability allows, Canada has tremendous untapped resources to back its currency without gouging its international neighbors.

Canada operates under the domino banking theory — that is, no bank can fail unless all banks fail — which is a remote situation indeed unless the entire world collapses.

Canada's major bank is The Royal Bank Of Canada, Head Office: The Royal Bank Of Canada Building, Place Ville Marie, Montreal, Canada.

This solid bank has over 1,100 branch banks from one end of Canada to the other. Impressive indeed.

Now here is where the U.S.A. tax haven seeker benefits.

Without leaving home or office, you can open either a Canadian or U.S. dollar deposit account. In the case of a U.S. dollar account, there is no with-holding tax made by the bank for the Canadian government. In case you want to convert your U.S. dollars to Canadian dollars and open a Canadian dollar account, the annual withheld rate is 15% of the interest due you. To give you some idea of the interest paid on Canadian dollar accounts, if the amount is only $1,000 or more on deposit for one year, the current rate is 8.5%. The 15% interest deduction is an expense you can expect credit for on your U.S. income tax return.

If you meet the balance requirements, you can open a U.S. dollar account in the Royal Bank, and there is no interest withheld. These situations are open to negotiations, and there are over 100 branch offices and representatives outside Canada. You can write to the Royal Bank for current interest percentage information. Or, ask them for the address of the nearest representative.

Any way you look at today's world, having part of your funds in Canada is as wise a move as you can make. Our neighbor Canada is a country blessed with abundant natural resources to help keep your money safer there — a true haven and capital protection country of the highest order.

Hong Kong

Hong Kong is as close to pure capitalism at this time as we can get — with a big plus. And that plus is full light industrial capacity to turn out well-made products. Certainly different from many off-shore tax havens that offer little more than attractive banking services.

Currency is freely exchanged. Daily rates are posted almost hourly and you can buy most any currency. Freely bring in and take out as much as you wish.

Especially for Americans, the fact that the official language for most business transactions is English eliminates difficult translations.

As we advised you earlier, you must check at the time you make your financial move to be up to the minute. Since many major U.S.A. banks have branches in Hong Kong, this is no problem. The foreign departments of domestic U.S.A. banks know or can find the answer to any of your overseas banking questions. The Bank of America or the First National City Bank, to name but two of the many good ones, will be glad to help you.

You can establish a limited company in Hong Kong — rather like the American corporation, by mail. You do not need to go to Hong Kong. There are many professional accountants qualified and able to serve you. You need no permission or clearance from the government to establish your limited company.

Three or four weeks is the normal time needed to register the company.

There is no Hong Kong capital gains tax. Nor is there a tax on gifts.

In addition, there are no tax dividends from your own company or from any other in which you might invest in Hong Kong.

The above benefits are enough to make any tax haven seeker take notice. But, when you add to this the high level of intelligence of the native Hong Kong work force, plus the open-handed welcome attitude of both the government and banking community, it is easy to understand why Hong Kong prospers. Just as many people who take advantage of all Hong Kong offers prosper too.

Belgium

When you strip away all the sensational publicity given to the value of Swiss bank accounts by novelists, movie and TV writers who teach us to equate a Swiss account with doubtful activities — when all this is swept away, you find you can get most all advantages with an account in Belgium as you can in Switzerland.

This small country in northwestern Europe supports a banking community in Brussels ready to serve you.

Numbered accounts, private accounts and con vertibility of funds are standard. In addition, you can depend on the stability of the industrious 10 million Belgians to maintain a stable economy to encourage the least fluctuations.

With ports on the North Sea, nestled between the Netherlands, West Germany, Luxembourg, and France, Belgium is ideally situated to encourage dependable transfers of funds when you need to make deals quickly.

And, when you have an account in Belgium, nary

an eyebrow is raised as it is when you have one or more Swiss accounts, which is a fact well worth remembering.

Bahamas

If you could select but one tax haven in the world, the Bahamas should be your first choice by far. The Bahamas come as close to being totally free of any government regulation and complete capital freedom as any place you can find in today's world. This sunny haven has all the best points of the other havens and none of the drawbacks. While it is an axiom that people in government power cannot resist the temptation to pass regulation after regulation, this stifling fault has so far not infected the wiser heads who oversee the laws of the Bahamas — thankfully.

This commonwealth is a self-governing former British colony (which became independent in 1973) of over 700 islands in the Atlantic Ocean, located between Florida and Haiti, with a population of more than 150,000, half of whom live in the capital city of Nassau. Because of the ideal year round climate and clear blue waters, the main industry is tourism.

And with a complete absence of taxes that wither capital in most other countries, it is fast becoming the world's leading tax haven.

Because of its historical roots, the official language is English. And the Bahamanian dollar is at parity with the U.S. dollar. Americans will have no trouble being understood or getting any financial information — probably much easier than facts in your own town. There is no capital gains tax, income tax, or corporation tax, and there is no interest tax.

Because of the importance of the Bahamas growing international financial position, there is an ample supply of talented professional accounting and legal services available to help you begin properly. It is not necessary for you to journey to the islands to establish the company or trust you wish to open. This can all be done by mail through your agent, who will be your attorney or accountant in the Bahamas. And when you are established properly and you remit your funds in U.S. dollars, any dividends, interest, and so on can be taken out in U.S. dollars.

Its quite simple, really. By making the proper application to buy real estate — which can be done by your agent, you can take out the money upon sale in your own currency. To encourage light industry there is a free trade zone on Grand Bahamas Island and it operates virtually tax free.

Gibraltar

A British crown colony occupying about 2 square miles on the Rock of Gibraltar, and comprising a town, seaport, and fortress dominating the Strait of Gibraltar, with a population of about 25,000.

It is assumed in this book that most Americans are more interested in establishing limited companies, trusts or partnerships in havens while continuing to live in America, rather than migrating and becoming a resident of the haven. Should you decide to live in Gibraltar, you will pay an income tax of 30% to 45%, depending on your gross income. And 30% on companies.

But when you are a non-resident and your company or trust is established in Gibraltar, and you have an "exempt" status, no tax will be due unless you bring the money into Gibraltar. Your legal advisor who sets up your Gibraltar entity will arrange the "exempt" status for you and explain well in advance what you must do to qualify for it and what you must do to maintain the status to legally avoid taxes — which is the whole purpose of any haven anyway.

A company can be formed in a matter of days once you are sure of what you want to do.

As we stated before, since Americans live in

such a big country, they seldom think beyond their borders as Europeans who must master several languages and criss cross borders in daily activities do. Living in a big land, it is natural to think in terms of only American state and federal tax laws, rather than international tax havens, where you can legally see your money grow faster.

Therefore, the purpose of this chapter is to call to your attention the tax havens that do exist. And some facts about them. With this opening information as a start, you can begin to add to your store of haven facts through your bank, accountant or attorney. And you can write to the embassy that represents the haven for more information. The embassy can either give you the information you want, or refer you to a government agency or bank in the haven for more information. Anyway you look at it, here is what you need to broaden your international financial outlook and see your capital increase.

British Virgin Islands

These are a group of about 100 islands, lying east of Puerto Rico in the West Indies, and divided into The British Virgin Islands, The Virgin Islands of the United States, including the islands of St. Thomas, St. John and St. Croix, with a combined area of 133 sq. miles, and with a population of about 35,000. Capital: Charlotte Amalie on St. Thomas. Like other havens in this section of the world, the men who govern the Virgin Islands see many advantages to developing their particular legal entity as a tax haven, since they certainly see other nearby havens doing very well.

In this haven, the currency is the U.S. dollar and the language is English.

As in other havens the level of accounting and legal proficiency is high. And, of course, you have international banking facilities. As for other taxes, there is no capital gains tax, and tax is levied only on income coming into the territory.

As with other havens, the company can be formed quickly.

MAJOR TYPES OF BUSINESS AND TAX TIPS THAT COULD SAVE YOU HUNDREDS OF DOLLARS THIS YEAR ALONE

Sub Chapter-S Corporations

This type of corporation chooses not to be taxed as a corporation, but passes along their gains and losses to the stockholders. They have the same benefits as a regular corporation as far as figuring income and expenses. However, any corporate loss is picked up directly by the stockholders.

The stockholders pay their personal tax on the corporate gain or loss even though the corporation doesn't pay any dividends.

The corporation pays no corporate income tax, but in some states there is a franchise tax — consult your tax accountant if you plan to use this type of business corporation.

Individual or Partnership

The owner of a business picks up, on his personal income tax return, the profits or losses of his business. However, the fringe benefits for employees such as life and hospitalization insurance, profit sharing, sick pay, etc., are denied to a sole owner or a partner, because they are not considered employees of the business.

The self-employed person can set up his own pension plans, but usually they offer less tax advantage then employee type plans.

In a particular type of business, the losses or gains are paid on the percent of ownership by each partner. Please remember, partnerships are not treated as taxable entities separate and apart from the owners.

Corporations

Regular corporations are considered separate taxpayers from the owner-stockholders. The corporation pays tax on its profits and uses its own losses as deductions. A stockholder of a corporation does not report his proportionate share of corporation gains or losses.

The stockholder is affected only when the corporation pays a dividend, or he sells his stock at a profit or loss, or the corporation goes out of business and the stock becomes worthless.

Also, a stockholder-owner who works for the corporation is considered an employee of the corporation. In addition, a one-man corporation can have employee benefit plans. The Treasury Department has approved a way for a one-man corporation to receive tax benefits of a pension or profit sharing plan.

You can qualify for the plan even though it covers only one single employee. However, there are stipulations and safeguards. One of the requirements is that you must provide coverage for any new people employed at a later date.

$$ How Charles R., from a Personal Investment, Reduces His Tax Bite

The IRS has ruled that an employee can contribute up to 10% of his or her salary in a Treasury-approved stock bonus or trust plan. This is a big saving if you are in a large income tax bracket. For instance, Charles R., the manager of a midwest pipeline, has earnings that have put him in the 42% tax bracket. The company has an approved benefit trust which allows him to contribute up to 10% of his salary.

On a salary of $25,000 a year, he puts up $2,500 of his own money. Here is how he benefits taxwise:

If Charles R. purchased bonds that yield 8% — after ten years his earned income would be $6,400 after taxes. But, if the trust could invest his money in the same bonds, his investment would now be worth $11,000 before taxes.

If Charles retires and draws his interest in a lump sum, his contribution to the plan (before 1974) would be taxed at capital gains rates, while the rest would receive the special 10-year averaging formula.

But that is not all. If Charles elects to draw his money out over a period of time instead of a lump sum, his tax will depend on his income over the years, which usually is much lower than his current bracket.

A LITTLE KNOWN ANGLE TO KEEP YOU IN A LOWER INCOME TAX BRACKET WHEN INCOME JUMPS

When you read or hear about the enormous salaries paid an athlete or an entertainer, you wonder what his tax bite will be. There is one angle that all high-priced individuals know. It is called "income averaging," but it also applies to individual business men, partners and executives. The income can be derived from large salaries, dividends, commissions, or large windfall profits.

Income averaging is a method of figuring income tax for the person who happens to have an unusually large income during his taxable year as compared to the previous four years.

It applies to any income except a few minor

items, and it also applies to large gambling wins or capital gains.

A taxpayer may increase tax savings by income averaging.

Here are a few examples of how to keep you in a lower income bracket using the income-averaging method.

1. *You, as an employee, are promoted to an executive position at triple your present salary.*

2. *A doctor or lawyer gets the largest fee of a lifetime.*

3. *You suddenly realize a short term capital gain.*

4. *If you own a closely held corporation and pay out large sums of money as dividends to yourself.*

5. *A salesman makes the biggest sale of his life and collects a large commission.*

6. *An executive receives an unexpected year end bonus.*

If you are eligible to use the income averaging angle, you should prepare Schedule "G," and add it to your tax return. But please remember, if this is your first year to file an income averaging return — it isn't a method to spread your income over a period of years — but to arrive at your tax rate for the current year.

As we mentioned, tax laws change. Always get professional help — you will be dollars ahead.

THE MAGIC ART OF
COMBINING BUSINESS AND
VACATION IN ONE TRIP —
TAX FREE

Every man owes it to himself to take a vacation at least once a year. And, as you gain freedom financially, you should take two or three. It takes you away from your business and gives your mind a chance to clear out the cobwebs from the daily routine of business.

However, if you are planning to combine your vacation and business into one trip, here are some tips to get you the maximum tax deductions for business expenses, while still on a pleasure trip.

A) If your trip is for vacation or pleasure — you can not deduct traveling expenses from your home to your destination. But, you can deduct the cost of side trips that pertain to your business. For instance, if you take your family to Los Angeles on vacation, and then you go to San Diego for a few days on business calls, you can deduct your expenses from Los Angeles to San Diego, but you can't deduct your expenses getting to Los Angeles in the first place.

B) If your trip is strictly for business, the entire expenses are deductible, regardless of whether you go by plane, automobile or ox cart.

Don't forget that all your meals, motel expenses and telephone calls are tax deductible if business related.

If you travel outside the continental United States for more than a week, and 25% of your time is for pleasure, you must pro-rate expenses, business and pleasure. Only the part allowed as business is tax deductible.

So, on your next business trip, why not enjoy a portion as a vacation.

HOW TO LEGALLY AVOID TAX ON PROFITS FROM SALE OF YOUR HOME

The old saying "Every man's home is his castle", should read "Every man's home is his capital gain". I find more and more families are selling their homes to take advantage of the large profits they have as equity.

But, if you sell your home and make a profit, you will have to report the profit and pay tax as a capital gain.

However, there are ways, if you qualify, to defer your tax payment until some future date, or you can avoid paying any tax at all.

One tax break which could eliminate all tax, or at least defer the tax, is the provision that you purchase or build another residence within a certain length of time.

Another good break is for the individual who is over 55 years old, which allows you complete tax exemption on the first $100,000 profit from the sale of your home. If you are nearing the age of 55, it would be well if you consulted your tax accountant to see if you can take advantage of this tax avoidance.

Please keep in mind that tax laws can change from year to year.

As we mentioned, you get a tax break if you replace your residence within a certain period of time. Under this provision you are taxed only to the extent that the sale price of your present home exceeds the price of your new residence. In other words, if your new home costs as much as your old house sold for, you have no tax to pay.

But that's not all. If you have reached the age of 55 before you sell your home, you may be able to qualify for complete exemption.

For example, your home cost you $30,000 and you sell for $40,000 which makes a net profit of $10,000. Then you purchase a new home for $40,000 you pay no tax on the $10,000 profit. The tax is deferred until you sell your new home. But, if you buy another residence, the tax is deferred as long as you replace your home within the required time limit.

Also, if you die before paying the deferred tax, the tax on the profit is wiped out and your heirs sell your property at the price it was worth at your death, they would not pay any tax at all.

There is one point we should remember. This tax break applies only to your principal residence. It does not apply to the Swiss chalet in the mountains, or the lakeside villa used for a summer resort.

However, the tax break isn't just limited to houses. Your principal residence could be a mobile home or a condominium. If you are planning to sell your principal residence, check out the tax breaks. They are in your favor and this could mean hundreds of dollars in tax savings.

HOW TO "GIVE IT AWAY — AND KEEP IT TOO" AND LEAVE MORE CASH IN YOUR POCKET

By taking advantage of available tax shelters, you can almost eliminate the bite taxes taken from your estate.

You are concerned with Federal Gift and Estate Tax. If your estate is of moderate size, you may be completely free of tax because the government itself has provided ways to help you lift the burden of taxes. For example:

Everyone gets, under present laws (subject to

change), a $60,000 exemption. Also, a married person receives benefits of a marital deduction in which you can leave up to half of your estate to your mate before the Federal tax applies.

There's only one thing to remember — taxes are graduated from 3% on the first dollar to 77% on ten million. Everyone falls within the range somewhere.

Your taxable estate is defined as the gross estate, less all deductions. It is comprised of everything you own — real estate, automobiles, cash in the bank — everything from the grandfather clock to your lawn mower.

However, you can give away some of your assets during your life, which will greatly reduce your estate taxes, with one exception known as "deathbed gifts." The rule is that with any gifts made three years prior to death, the government assumes they were made in contemplation of death, and would be subject to tax unless you have proof otherwise.

As we mentioned, everyone gets an exemption of $60,000, which is not subject to Federal tax — but if your estate is $75,000, then $15,000 would be taxable.

Funeral expenses are exempt as are expenses in settling your estate, mortgages, or any other debts you may owe are subtracted from your gross estate. Charitable gifts are also deductable.

Before you make a gift to a charity in your will, make sure it qualifies for a deduction. The law is very specific about this. You may contribute to religious, scientific, educational and charitable organizations that do not attempt to influence legislation. You can give to the Red Cross, Boy Scouts, churches, hospitals and even to the United States Government, or you may wish to contribute by giving land to your city for a park or recreation facility, in which case the value of the land would be deductable.

If you would like to avoid paying any estate tax

at all — give it all away. The federal estate laws limit your deductions for charities unless you give it all — then you pay no estate tax.

The super rich often use this method to save on taxes: Andrew Mellon left his entire estate to a trust known as the A. W. Mellon Educational and Charitable Trust. This method of giving it away saved him approximately 67 million on a hundred million dollar estate.

You don't have to be super rich to set up a trust that will provide an income for your family. It is simple. The interest income goes to your family, while the principal goes to charity. For example, if you are a widow or widower with an estate of $250,000, and you want to leave it in a way that a son or daughter will have financial security, and in the event of their death that it will go to your favorite charity, there are two ways you could handle this.

First: If you leave it all to your child, the estate tax would be approximately $50,000 and your child would receive $200,000, which could earn 7% interest. This would give them an annual income of $14,000.

Second: If you left the estate in a trust with the interest income going to your son or daughter — and on their death, the principal goes to your designated charity — the IRS allows you a deduction on the amount that you gave to the charity. This lowers the tax to $12,000 which leaves $238,000 in your trust fund. With the same 7% return, the annual income would be $16,660 which gives your heir an additional $2660 annual income.

Consult the trust department of your local bank, they will be glad to handle the paper work so you can "give it away and keep it too" and still have cash in your pocket.

HOW TO GIVE YOUR WIFE OR
HUSBAND $1,000,000 —
TAX FREE

The easiest way to lower your estate tax is to simply give away most of your property during your life time. Naturally, this reduces your gross estate and the amount of taxes due.

But you might ask, "Aren't you overlooking the gift tax?" No. It is a wise move because under our present estate tax laws (subject to change), gift tax rates are only three-fourths the amount of Federal estate taxes. In other words, if your net estate is $50,000 your tax would be $7,000. If you gave it as a taxable gift, the gift tax would be only $5250 — You save $1750.

There are special tax free allowances for married couples. For instance: Half of any gift from husband to wife (or vice versa) is tax free as a marital deduction.

Using this legal formula, it is possible for a married couple to give away $1,000,000 over a span of 20 years — *tax free.*

But please remember, tax free allowances apply only to the gift tax, with the exception of formal contributions to charities, religious or educational organizations. Also, don't overlook the fact that the gift tax is paid by the donor, not the one who receives the gift.

People have been known to get around the gift tax by a fictitious sale. Let's say you sell your Mother-in-law an acre of land for $1,000 — but the government has it appraised at $10,000 — They will consider the difference of $9,000 as a gift, subject to tax on your part.

Anyone who tries to evade taxes is asking for trouble. Take advantage of tax shelters available, but don't try to walk a tight wire.

Here are a few taxwise dollar saving tips:

1. *Have your attorney review your estate plan once a year.*

2. Keep your plan flexible to allow for financial gains.
3. Make a will today — both husband and wife.
4. Get the best estate planner you can afford.
5. Don't make the mistake of letting a friend or relative be executor of your estate — name a bank or a trust company.
6. Never assume your estate is too small — find out your net worth today.
7. Don't overlook the advantage of giving away property rather than letting it accumulate into a large estate.
8. Always get professional legal and tax advice.

You owe it to your family to get professional estate tax advice. It could mean thousands of dollars when they need it the most.

So, take full advantage of all legal tax shelters that have been made available to you.

After all, its your money.

CHAPTER TWELVE

PLAIN MILLIONAIRE TALK ABOUT YOUR MONEY

The saying "a rolling stone gathers no moss" may be true for stones, but it isn't true with a dollar. A rolling dollar gathers dollars. You must keep your money turning and must roll it over several times a year to increase your percentage of profits.

For example, the newspaper boy who delivers your daily paper is the perfect example of an entrepreneur and a capitalist. He keeps his money rolling. Let's say he begins his morning with $10. He buys 250 papers and sells them for $25. He does this twice a day, and when he checks his receipts at the end of the day, he has $50. What has he accomplished? He has sold 500 papers and made a $30 profit.

He is a true entrepreneur. He does his own labor and furnishes his own money — and above all, he isn't a speculator, because he can get his money back on all papers he doesn't sell. He is the finest example of keeping your money turning. He makes approximately $5,000 a year with a $10 investment, and, of course, with a lot of leg work thrown in.

But that's not all. Compare him to a jeweler who has a $100,000 inventory and whose sales are $100,000 a year. The newsboy turns his money over 600 times a year; the jeweler only once.

This brings us to another great law — The Law Of Finance. It isn't how much money you have, but how many times you roll it over. Ask yourself the question, "How many times do I turn my money over?" Do you move it once a year, quarterly, weekly, or daily? Every millionaire knows this law of finance and works it to perfection.

There are two plants in Oklahoma City. One has about $2,500,000 in operating capital and 500 employees; the other has about $500,000 and 100 employees. They both made approximately the same net profit last year. Why? Because the smaller plant turns its money over three times, while the other firm turns its capital once.

The man who owns a donut shop can do business on 1/10 the money as our jeweler friend, because he can turn his flour into donuts quickly and his donuts into cash. He can sell his whole batch in one day.

One reason why some entrepreneurs make such little money is that they keep their money tied up. For instance:

1. *They have too much inventory not moving*

2. *They have too many high priced machines idle*

3. *They have too many buildings housing too much raw material*

Never overlook this fact — Idle goods and idle machinery equals idle money.

I have talked to businessmen seeking business loans where half their capital was tied up in dead weight, while the other half did the work. Never once did they think to sell or put into motion the money they had tied up in goods or inventory.

If you wish to deal like a millionaire, you must learn this one fact — You can not make money out of possessions unless the price goes up. The value of anything depends on its use, not what you paid for it. *Let me repeat* — Value is based on use, not what you paid for it.

This includes everything you own, if you are going to make a profit. It can be a machine or land. Many a businessman has a "white elephant" on his hands simply because he didn't heed this rule. Just because something is high-priced doesn't mean it will make money.

Better to have an engine with one chicken power that runs than a 500 h.p. diesel that won't start.

Better to take $5,000 and start it rolling than have $100,000 tied up in dead merchandise.

In this chapter, "Plain Millionaire Talk About Your Money," I would like you to remember that our free enterprise system is based on exchange. Money for merchandise, merchandise for money. Making a profit on the exchange is the secret of "dealing" like a millionaire.

Here is a case of two furniture stores in the same town. Each store handles the same brand of reclining rocker. One store would put a high mark up on his chair of $500, and would sell maybe one a year. The other store priced theirs at $300, and would sell one a month. He then buys again, repeats the process, and sells twelve chairs a year. Now, lets say the cost of each chair was $200. Simple arithmetic tells us that the store with the high mark up has a profit of $300 for the year, while the store with a rapid turnover of chairs has a profit of $1,200.

You can see why one store can double its trade, while the store across the street barely makes ends meet.

The huge discount stores understand this principal, yet few entrepreneurs ever grasp the idea in a lifetime.

You must learn that 1½ % per month is more profitable than 12% per year. Your bank or finance companies know this.

You could liken money to brains. Years ago it was believed a man with a large brain was smarter than a man with a small one, but that is untrue. If the big-sized brain equaled intelligence, we would have baboons running the country.

Regardless of the size of your brain, if you don't use it, you are in the class of the stupid. This accounts for the reason that some businessmen are successful and others are going broke.

Almost every time I ask a businessman what he needs most, he says "more money." Wrong! What he needs is to turn over what money he has twice as fast. Always look at your store as a temporary stop over for merchandise, not a warehouse for goods.

You must keep rolling your money — put every dollar to work — don't let them sleep on the job. Roll your dollar so fast that it will gather other little dollars and bring them back to you.

WHAT MAKES THE BANKING
INDUSTRY TICK — TO
YOUR BENEFIT

To understand banking, you must first understand what money is. Money is nothing more than a promise to pay, which means if you accept a dollar for our services, you have the assurance that someone else will, in the future, take the dollar and give you full value for it. All it amounts to is confidence in a transaction, and the dollar beats trading in beans and beads.

Our society has evolved into a highly technical banking system, using paper money. Sometime in the future a checkless society will evolve, using only plastic cards. This will be necessary to speed the billions of transactions that pass through the banking system.

But, please remember, no matter how sophisticated banking becomes, banks are still in business for one reason — *profit.*

Many small town banks are still family-owned enterprises, just like the grocery store down the street. The grocer is selling goods; the banker is selling service. The grocer stocks his shelves with groceries; the banker with money in the vault.

For the use of your money (a depositor), you are paid interest or you receive a credit to your passbook. One major difference between the banker and other businessmen is that he is highly regulated by the federal government in order to protect what you have on deposit and make sure the bank's investments are sound and beneficial to you and the community.

The federal government's close control of the banks is a blessing, but it often hinders competition in a free enterprise system, especially in regard to the control of interest on savings accounts and the relation to the amount of interest charged on loans.

I am not going to debate banking regulations, but will give you an insight into the three banking systems that are available to you.

Commercial Banks

Commercial banks are the real backbone of the monetary system. Without them, we would be back to the bean and beads system of barter. They are aggressive and never hesitate to borrow good ideas from their competitors, the mutual savings and loan institutions.

They will immediately adopt good tactics that will draw depositors, such as the "Golden Pass Book" or computing of interest daily to increase your earnings on deposits.

If you could call banks enterpreneurs, the commercial bank would stand heads above the rest of its competitors. Its investments are more diversified, and since they are less regulated, their loans to you or big business can often earn them three times the amount of interest of mutual banks and savings and loans.

The commercial banks keep a watchful eye on savings and loans and mutual banks, and would deal them a death blow like a cat on a mouse if they were not regulated by the federal government.

With their awesome reserves of capital, they could easily put their competitors out of business with higher yields on offerings — or they could immediately raise the interest paid on deposits if the federal government would allow it.

This puts the federal regulators in a precarious position. The public cries for increased earnings on their deposits and banks' incomes are soaring. This has caused many investors to pull their money out of their banks and place it in out of country banks that have a higher yield on savings.

However, the Comptroller of Currency and the Congressional Banking Committees know the banking industry must be monitored at all times. As mentioned, without controls, it would siphon the money from the savings and loans and would hinder the housing industry, which greatly affects our economic growth.

Many people criticize banks, but without them, we couldn't enjoy the freedom of exchange of goods

and services for money, which has enabled millionaires to flourish in the United States and made possible the opportunity for you to "deal" like one.

Mutual Savings Banks

How they arrived at the name "mutual" is a mys-
tery of the century, because they certainly don't be-
long to you and me. However, in highly technical
wording, you as a depositor, are in a sense a "stockholder," but you have little to say in management,
policy on interest payments, or who is elected chairman of the board. The depositors have no control
whatsoever over the lending or investment policy.

The wide difference in mutual banks' investment activity and the amount of dividends (interest)
paid to stockholders (depositors) has allowed them to
build a huge surplus of money. In addition, they have
become the most aggressive of all their competitors.

In every bank lobby, you see all kinds of gimmicks
to attract depositors. Free gifts to new depositors
(later in this chapter I will show how to take advantage of this offer for your own benefit), grace periods
on loans, high interest on certificates of deposit,
Christmas clubs, and so on. Often, their lobby looks
more like a discount store than a bank.

Government banking regulations allow the mutual to pay a slightly higher rate of interest on savings
than its competitor, the commercial bank. With this
tool, it sets up its advertising. It loudly proclaims its
"high interest rates," and claims that "your money is
safer here." Often, the public never knows that other
institutions offer the same services at better rates.

The question comes to mind, "Why does the federal government allow a mutual to pay a higher
dividend than a commercial bank?" There is a little
"kicker" to the priviledge — the government requires
that they invest the majority of depositors' money in

home mortgage loans, which, we must admit, is in the public interest.

This has made mortgage money available to many individuals who have the dream of owning their own home.

The mutual bank has established its place in our complex monetary system by furnishing money to stimulate construction of homes and furnish mortgage money to the buyer.

Savings and Loan Associations

Since the founding of savings and loan associations in the 1950s, they have been a thorn in the side of the mutual banks. They offer the same services, and their prime reason for existence is to invest in home mortgages, apartments and commercial buildings. They are so nearly alike in function to mutuals that they are often called "kissing cousins".

The savings and loans multiplied so rapidly that they pulled away many long time customers of the mutuals. The mutuals could see the handwriting on the wall and established a campaign to bring the savings and loans into their way of thinking and doing business.

Today, it would be hard to tell them apart. They pay the same dividends and offer the same services. They both have the same objective — *profit* — and both stimulate home building and buying.

The F.D.I.C. and Your Money

If I didn't mention the Federal Deposit Insurance Corporation, (F.D.I.C.) in this section of plain millionaire talk about your money, I would be short-changing you.

The F.D.I.C. as its name implies, is an insurance corporation. It operates on the same principal as a life insurance company. The insurance companies are betting on the fact that everyone doesn't die at the same time. The F.D.I.C. is betting that all banks don't go broke on the same day.

With the soundness of the American banking system, this would occur only if the capitalist system ceased to exist or a national disaster occurred.

If there was a large scale closing of banks, the F.D.I.C. is so closely tied in with our monetary system, that they would swim together. They have a powerful backup system — the Federal Reserve and the United States Treasury. You would suffer only a temporary inconcenience until you were paid by the F.D.I.C.

I know of one bank that was closed because of mismanagement, and the depositors were all reimbursed. However, it took several months to reconcile the banks records, which would indicate that you should keep your money in two or three different banks so you could have ready access to funds in the event that one was closed.

Let me repeat — your money is safer in your local bank than under the mattress where thieves may break in and steal it.

HOW TO "BREAK" THE BANK GIVEAWAY PROGRAMS

There are days when your bank or savings and loan lobbys look like a toy store, with prizes from electric blankets to piggy banks that will gobble your money with the flick of the tongue.

I even know of one savings and loan that gives green stamps.

There was a time when you could open an account one day, get your prize, withdraw your money the next day and repeat the process across the street at another bank. But the banks could see what was happening and now impose a few rules, limiting the giveaway program to openings of new branches or on special holidays.

When you visit your bank, inquire as to the day when there will be a giveaway program. The gift will often add to your earnings.

But that's not all. Here is a guide that will help you determine if the gift is worth the investment.

There are regulations that control the value of gifts. For example:

Deposit amount	Approximate retail price of gift
$50	$5.00
$500	$10.00
$5,000	$20.00

Please remember to check the approximate retail price of gifts. This is how you can determine if the minimum deposit will earn the more valuable gift. You can see from the chart that you would be dollars ahead if you made ten $500 deposits instead of one $5,000 deposit.

Using this chart, a $50 deposit gets you a retail gift of $5, which would add a 10% value to your deposit.

Here is a tip — open your account with the least deposit required and you might encourage all the members of your family to open an account at the same bank or savings and loan company. Everyone would benefit.

One word of caution — you should find out if there is a time limit on withdrawal without a penalty, because it could be greater than the cost of your gift.

In addition, find out whether you can later change the account to a high interest account, such as a certificate of deposit.

Keep alert to all giveaway programs. It's just like a "Break the Bank Show," with you controlling the prizes.

HOW AN INSIDE BANK SECRET CALLED "FLOATS" CAN DOUBLE YOUR INTEREST INCOME

To make this little trick of the trade work, you must have a savings account known as a day of deposit to day of withdrawal account. This is a simple savings account that allows the bank to transfer a portion of your savings to your checking account, to cover any overdrafts that could occur This enables you to keep a small checking account balance while your funds are drawing interest until transferred to cover any checks. One suggestion is to leave your savings account pass book with one of the officers of the bank or someone in bookkeeping that can readily make transfers, to keep you from having to pay any charge on any checks with insufficient funds.

In every business — manufacturing, retail or sales — there are tricks of the trade. The same is true of banking. Floats are one trick that you can take advantage of and increase the interest earned on your money.

A "float" is a banking term that defines a deposit made by check whose funds have not been collected by the receiving bank. The majority of banks, due to the high paper load of checks and the slowness of the mails, will credit interest to a check the day it is received, even if the check hasn't cleared the issuing bank.

This is best operated between two banks that are a good distance apart. For example: A Los Angeles bank and a New York bank may offer a 10-day grace period. Your savings account in your home town bank should be a day of deposit to day of withdrawal account.

Then, you withdraw a teller's check and mail it for deposit in Los Angeles no later than the 10th of the month. The deposit will earn interest from the 1st of the month on the uncollected money. If it takes a week before the funds are withdrawn from your day of deposit to day of withdrawal savings account, you are earning 20 days of free interest every month.

The "float" is the nearest thing to double interest that you can get from your savings account.

$$ How Jeanne G. Amassed $100,000 with $20 a Week

Right here, let me say something to you — I am not a pessimist when I say that no man ever became wealthy through the savings plan of a bank by salting away a certain amount each week.

I will say that there is no better way to train yourself than saving money. When you save a pre-determined amount of your weekly pay check, and do so for a number of years, it becomes a habit. This means that you learn to live within your income, and later, when you have your own business, you have learned the value of having a cash reserve.

Start today. Put a fixed amount in a savings account. If you can't put in $20 a week, put $5. If that's too much, put something you can live with. By all means, start today.

Later on, your balance will grow and grow, and you will receive a certain thrill in watching the interest increase in your savings pass book.

You could accumulate a fortune like Jeanne G., who regularly put away $20 a week for twenty-five years, and with the growing power of compound interest, she retired with a tidy sum of $100,000.

I recently read of another lady who amassed over $250,000 using this formula. All it takes is patience, time and a good habit of saving each week. Your savings are insured by the F.D.I.C., so there is no risk involved.

You may say, "I don't have a weekly salary because I am self-employed." But, we would venture to say that after you have met all salaries and operating expenses, you could add another fixed charge each month — A "Pay Yourself Plan." I agree, it is a hard thing to draw a large amount from your profits at the end of the year, but you can pay yourself first at the end of the month — which would be easy and hardly missed from your business.

Every man who is self-employed should figure what percentage of his cash receipts each month is profit. Then, he should pay himself a fixed amount and deposit it in a savings account, just as if he were earning a salary from a large corporation.

There is a sum between one dollar and one thousand dollars that you can take out each week or month, without affecting the overall operation of your business.

Take a tip from Frank Blalock, a supermarket operator. He figures his previous years profits as a guide to the amount to pay himself. For example: If his store's net profit was $6,000 each month from $100,000 gross sales, he knows that 6% of his cash receipts are profits. He then pays himself 5% each month, to be deposited in his savings account, which leaves 1% to accumulate in his business — which is a bonus he pays himself at the end of the year.

It makes no difference if you are salaried or in business for yourself — you can amass a fortune using the savings plan method.

I could furnish charts and figures to show you the dollar amounts that would accumulate over a given number of years at certain rates of interest, but if you are like me — statistics are boring. So, go to your banker and have him get out his little desk computer and figure how much you could earn in twenty-five years on the amount you wish to deposit each week in a savings account. You will be surprised at the amount of money you can accumulate with good savings habits.

The savings habit will not only amass a fortune, it will teach you the difference between principal and interest. It teaches you that when you buy something for $100 that it is worthless, it not only cost you a hundred bucks, but also causes you to lose the amount of interest it would have accumulated in your passbook.

Every banker knows that a person who doesn't have a savings account is living beyond his means, and sooner or later (and most often sooner), he will be without a job or suffer a business loss.

Believe me, the world is a mighty lonely place to live when you haven't anything to fall back on. And, by the same token, if you have money in the bank, it's a beautiful and happy place to be after all.

HOW TO CREATE BIG MONEY
FAST FROM DEBT

From the title of this book, *How To "Deal" Like a Millionaire and Get Rich on Borrowed Money,* you can see that debt is involved. But please remember, all millionaires borrow heavily, most successful businessmen rely on debt to operate their business or plants, and don't forget, even our government operates on credit. I know for a fact that if it were not for debts, most banks would have to close their doors. Banks survive because they know that loans are as much a factor in your business as employees or merchandise.

It is also known that a man who is in debt puts in longer hours and better planning to make a success of his life than a person who is complacent and doesn't owe a dime.

Money has a fixed amount in the matter of how much it can earn in interest. This fixed value can be 8% or 10%, whatever the case may be. However, a person who deals like a millionaire can make 15%,

25%, or 50% on this same money, with a little hard work and planning.

Therefore, there are golden opportunities for the entrepreneur to borrow money at 10%, and take that money and his own energy and earn 100% or greater.

You can afford to pay the prime rate for money. The banks, savings and loans, and the mutual banks know what can be accomplished with debt.

They have helped millions of people live in their own home because they chose to go into debt. How many people do you think would own a home if they had to save up the purchase price? Very few.

The farmer goes into debt in the spring and reaps his crops in the fall, and you can liken an entrepreneur to the farmer. Very few men have much money in their springtime, or youth — the majority reap their harvest or fortunes in the fall, or later years.

You could say that up to 50 years old was the debt period — that up to fifty, a man pays interest.

After fifty, he begins to collect interest.

Go into debt, borrow money, and make the borrowed money work hard and make you rich. Then, when you have reached the fall years of life, let your surplus wealth earn you money in sound investments.

I have noted over the years that most bankers are over 50 years old, and that entrepreneurs who borrow money are under fifty. Nature has favored the younger man with the fire of ambition and ability, and has endowed the middle-aged man with experience and good judgment.

Let me say again, debt without rhyme or reason will eventually lead to bankruptcy. Don't rush into debt to make a killing in a wild scheme.

Set your goals and take one step at a time. You will find that most fortunes are made from thirty to sixty years of age.

From twenty to thirty, you are building a solid

foundation to create big money fast — from debt.

Debt is a great incentive to riches. Use it wisely.

HOW TO TURN PLASTIC CREDIT CARDS INTO INSTANT CASH — LEGALLY

Right here, let me say this to you — don't take those little plastic cards in your pocket or purse lightly. They are known as "plastic money," and are a powerful weapon for obtaining instant cash legally.

Much has been said about credit cards. Their critics claim they pave the road to bankruptcy; their booster clubs claim they are a boom to our system and a convenience for their owners.

But, not enough has been said about the inside tricks that can be employed to make money, or point out the additional earnings you can receive from extended credit.

Credit cards come in various sizes and colors — but the latest trend is for all to fit the same machine. The most popular at present are the Visa and Master-Charge, and you can walk into almost any bank in your town and pick one up. You obtain instant credit at over a million outlets world wide.

I also have what is known as the "upper crust" credit cards. These are the Carte Blanche, Diner's Club and American Express. They carry a little prestige because of the annual membership fee, and they are issued to a select few. But, with a good paying record you may readily obtain one.

One of the features of the plastic credit card is the provision of the grace period. It usually takes 30 days from the date of charge to the time of billing. Often, if paid within a certain time limit, there is no service charge — which is the same as interest-free money.

Here is what happens. When you make a purchase or a charge using "plastic money," as I mentioned, the invoice arrives in approximately 30 days, and you have up to 25 additional days to pay. With a little mental arithmetic, you can see that you have 55 days use of the credit card time (money to you), because this is money you could have in a savings account drawing 55 days interest.

But, that's not all. If your purchases are made out of state, your time lapse could run up to 90 days. Overseas purchases can be delayed six months or longer before you receive a statement. Your credit card is a tool you must learn to use.

It is a big gun in your arsenal of weapons to help keep your money in a day of deposit to day of withdrawal savings account.

The most closely guarded secret of plastic money is the cash advance feature. Many credit card companies advertise this feature of their card — but what they don't advertise is multiple card ownership.

Very few people know they can have more than one card issued by the same company as long as the issuing bank is different. Apply for as many Master-Charge and Visa cards as you can obtain. If you are thinking along with me, you can see that with five Visa cards and five MasterCharge cards with a credit limit of $1,000, you have ten thousand dollars available to you for any golden opportunity that could come along. You have your own full range of personal loans — instant cash — legally, by simply signing your name.

"Plastic money" is challenging cash as a medium of exchange. Don't carry just one or two credit cards — carry a bundle. Buy now and pay later — keep your cash intact in a savings account drawing interest, which is the central theme of making money.

Robert Winkler, a V.P. of a neighborhood bank, has developed a new idea for the use of his credit cards. He has a wallet filled with almost every credit card available but he never uses them.

Robert has learned from many of his retail customers that there is a certain amount of resistance to accepting a credit card over cash. Retailers not only pay a fee to the issuing card company, but it often takes days to get reimbursed for credit card sales, and the volume of record keeping involved in the transaction is increased.

So, that is why Robert can negotiate for a discount when he pays cash. For example, you could say, "Mr. Retailer, we both know you have to pay a 5% to 10% service charge on my purchase. Why don't we split the difference and have you give me a 2½ % or 5% discount and I will pay cash. You pocket the difference, I get a discount and we both make money."

If you are making large purchases, you could trade off several dollars with the merchant. If he doesn't want to deal, try his competitor. Your chances will be 100 times greater if you make the proposition before you buy.

Use your plastic money. It is ready for instant use to put dollars in your pocket — legally.

HOW TO SPOT THE STRING TIED TO EVERY MONEY-MAKING PROPOSITION

It would be unfair to you if we didn't, at this point, tell you there is a string tied to every money-making proposition, regardless of who is involved. Believe me, it is to your benefit to look for the string before opening your wallet to any proposition made to you.

By dealing like a millionaire, you are going to attract all kinds of people with money-making ideas. So, that is why, when a stranger approaches and offers to do something for you, to let you in on the ground floor of a golden opportunity, or he tells you he is looking out for your interests, you can rest assured there is a string tied to his offer. And, 99% of the time, it is his interest he is looking after, not yours. Don't jump at the chance of an offer to get something for nothing. This is the biggest string of all. In fact, the string could be the size of a rope and you could hang yourself.

Please remember this, in the money making world, people are selfish. Everyone is looking out for his own interest, and if he is concerned about your interest, it is because it will benefit him the greatest.

This is a fact of life, and you must recognize this if you are to be successful in the art of dealing like a millionaire.

Don't run ahead to sign a contract with a stranger — many have smooth tongues. Walk, until you have found the string. Believe me, there is one. Find it before committing yourself to any kind of proposition that requires you to put up any cash in advance. You will be ahead of the game if you are cautious where the interest of others is involved.

Often, the string is on the up and up — but it is always to your advantage to find the string and see where it is tied.

Believe this simple truth — there is a string tied to every deal, and you must spot it before you hand over your hard earned money.

HOW TO PICK ASSOCIATES
THAT WILL LEAD YOU
QUICKLY TO BIG MONEY

"Water seeks its own level," "Birds of a feather flock together," "A man is known by the company he keeps." These are pure and simple truths. Who you associate with is of great importance to an entrepreneur. If you want to make money, if you want to deal like a millionaire, go where the money is being made. Mix and mingle with people who are getting rich.

The individual who spends his time at neighborhood poker parties or bending elbows at the local bar, can not think big money. There is no way he can hide the practices that rub off from this type of associate. He soon talks and acts the part of his pals and is soon dubbed with the title of a "good fellow."

It isn't hard to spot a "good fellow." He is always around where the noisy crowds hang out. He is quick to spend his salary or income for the drinks or the dinners, and in his own mind he is having a good time. By his actions, he is a "good fellow."

Test this truth — go to any club or bar and you will see the good fellow. Everyone calls him a good fellow because they are all good fellows together.

This type of person is always working for someone else, and then, only long enough to draw a pay check so he can go back and join his "birds of a feather" crowd to continue his role of a good fellow.

When this person dies, he is often broke. All the other good fellows have to chip in to bury him. The only people who show up for the funeral are the good fellows, and all the preacher can say about the deceased is, "Well, he was a good fellow."

The successful entrepreneur is like the honey bee — he stores up his money, for he knows he will soon create an opportunity to build up his reserve of cash for the day when he will achieve financial independence.

Make it your business never to be referred to as a "good fellow." Many people seem to think the words "good fellow" cover over the mistakes and faults of a person. They try to excuse him by saying, "Well, he was a good fellow, anyhow."

But, please remember there isn't a bank in the

country that will loan you money on the recommendation that you are a good fellow. It takes character to borrow money from the bank.

Character is credit with your banker, and you must pick associates that have character and money-making ideas that will help you to reach your goals.

How will a man ever improve his golf game if he always picks associates he can beat. He may satisfy his ego back at the club house, knowing he has won a game, but will he improve his own if he continues to play with inferiors? His golf game plan will begin to deteriorate, and soon he will be unable to beat anyone.

To be a winner, you must pick associates who have an uplifting influence on you.

Mix with your superiors in matters of money-making and you will pick up their way of thinking. Soon you will be out in front, with everything under your control.

Hitch your money wagon to a star and shun all associates who tend to pull you down. Your chances to deal like a millionaire will be a thousand times greater if you pick associates who will quickly lead you to the big money.

NOW THAT YOU HAVE IT, "GIVE IT — NEVER LEND IT"

It would be unfair to you if I didn't say a few things about the pitfalls of lending money to friends. There is an age old saying "Give it — never lend it."

No truer words were ever spoken when it comes to lending money. You should frame these words and place them on your desk as a reminder to protect what you have earned.

If some kindly person had taken me aside and told me these things twenty-five years ago, I would not only have saved a lot of money, but would have kept several friends as well.

As a banker, let me say right here — leave the money-lending to the banks, finance company and pawn broker. They have the expertise and knowledge on how to do it — you don't. They have the tools to collect — you haven't. They are in business for a profit, but when you lend you neither give nor invest — you never receive a thank you or a profit.

The day that it is known that you have money, regardless if you made it on your own or if you inherited it, you will find you have a new set of problems.

Here come the leeches — they seem to come out of the woodwork. I could make a list of leeches or spongers a mile long. They come in all shapes and sizes, from the wino on skid row to the preachers in their $300 suits. They arrive as friends, relatives or total strangers. They can be women as well as men. Some are honest, while others are outright thieves. Some will be deserving, others will not.

The pretty woman walking the streets — the silver-tongued con man — close friends — relatives you never heard of — all come with their hands out. Some approach with good intentions, but all with their eye on your wallet.

I know one man in Tulsa, Oklahoma, who had a nervous breakdown when he learned his own son had bled his business like a common thief.

There is no advanced technology to detect a leech or a free-loader, but there is a visual method. You can recognize one when he opens his mouth — and asks you to transfer some of your money from your pocket to his.

Every entrepreneur who is a hustler is surrounded by hangers-on, all waiting like vultures to steal what he has. As soon as you have money in the bank, don't become calloused to everyone, but you must learn to say "NO."

It is easier to make money than to keep it — ask any rich man. It requires boldness to accumulate money, but it requires ten times the effort to keep it intact.

This is why most wealthy people keep to themselves — they have to be on guard at all times. No matter how much money you have (it could be one thousand or one million dollars) all could be lost in a matter of minutes if you are caught off guard.

I know of a man who sold his business for $200,000 and moved to Los Angeles. In less than six months, the leeches had left him broke.

There just isn't a limit to the greed of a sponger — the more you lend, the more he wants. He is never satisfied. If you wish to keep your money, always *give* or *lend* out of your *interest income* or your earnings — always keep your capital intact and working.

Here is a word of caution that many bankers will never tell. Never, never endorse or co-sign a note for anyone — not even your own brother. I have seen good, honest hard-working men lose their business and jobs because they had to pay off notes after their friend had skipped town and left them to pay off large loans they had guaranteed.

You should never have a joint banking account with anyone — not even your wife. I have seen partners with joint checking accounts, where one withdrew all the funds and lost them in some wild scheme.

Right here, let me say this about wives — a good wife is capable of handling her own bank account. The man who has a wife with the same goals in life as himself, has a guarantee that he will be successful. But, pity the man who has a wife that is a hanger-on. No matter how smart or how strong, he will never make it. His goals are doomed from the start.

There are more divorces, arguments, and kill-ings over money than any other single factor.

Keep your money out of all personal involve-ments, for nothing brings out the worst in people than a difference of opinion about money.

If a friend hits you up for a loan, ask him why he doesn't go to his banker. If he tells you he is in a jam, whatever you do, don't lend him any money. Do him a favor, buy a small interest in his business. If he needs a thousand dollars, buy a thousand dollars interest in his business. You are now an investor and you have a right to say how he runs his business and a right to share in the profits. And, you have saved a friend.

If his business fails, you stand a chance of get-ting part of your money back and still keeping your friendship.

But that's not all, a man that tries to borrow from friends is usually unreliable — most self-sufficient men don't ever let their friends know they need money.

There is a certain type of leech in every city — a man who never pays his debts. He takes life easy and tries to get everything he can without working. He may be well educated, but he is a beggar. He is al-ways out of cigarettes and says, "Loan me ten dol-lars till next week." He is nothing more than a time waster and a loafer. He does not have the nerve to steal, but this type takes more from friends than any thief.

There is a strange fact about loaning money. Even if you lend to a best friend, you run the risk of losing a friendship. No one likes a lender. When you loan a friend money, you are no longer his buddy — you become a loan shark. The debt places a burden on him and he blames you for his plight, especially if he is unable to repay.

There is a law of nature — friendship cannot

exist between superiors and inferiors, it only exists between equals.

If a person asks you for money, he needs more than just money — never forget that.

Speaking on a moral level, "If you should give more than you do — then give only to those who are trying to help themselves."

A FINAL WORD

Now that the book, *How to "Deal" Like a Millionaire and Get Rich on Borrowed Money* is drawing to a close — I would like to say I have enjoyed sharing these money-making ideas with you.

In going through my files, searching my memory and referring to my notes of many years in the banking and lending industry, I have learned along with you. It has given me an opportunity to put much of what has contributed to my financial success down in writing, to aid you in a country where millionaires are made every day.

I envy the opportunity ahead of you — the chance to start or expand your own business or investment program, the chance to see the change in your life as you begin to make big money through your own efforts and abilities. It is a thrill you will never tire of.

Your success in making money could come faster than you think. It depends on how fast you make your start.

For years, I have believed that there are people with the ability to deal like millionaires. In fact, I am often appalled at the time and effort a person puts into a job or project and how little they are paid in relation to what they could make in a business or investment program of their own, with less effort and less time.

How are they going to learn? I don't know — but I do know I have pointed the way for *you* with this book. So, hopefully, you can now make a proper start. From this point, *it is up to you.* Who, more than yourself, has the right to decide how much money you make. It is your life and no one else's. Be happy, gain freedom.

Stop wasting precious years wishing and waiting. Make your move *now,* and above all, get on the road to dealing like a millionaire and getting rich on borrowed money.

You have what you need to make a start — *right here in this book.*

INDEX